Denkart Europa

Schriften zur europäischen Politik, Wirtschaft und Kultur | 24

The series is edited by ASKO EUROPA-STIFTUNG, Saarbrücken and
Europäische Akademie Otzenhausen gGmbH.

Hartmut Marhold [ed.]

Europe under Stress

Internal and External Challenges for the EU
and its Member States

2nd, Enlarged Edition 2017

 **Nomos**

These Policy Papers have been published online between September 2014 and July 2015 by the Research Department of the Centre international de formation européenne (CIFE), with the financial support of the European Commission.

 Centre international
de formation européenne

© Coverpicture: fotolia.com

The Deutsche Nationalbibliothek lists this publication in the
Deutsche Nationalbibliografie; detailed bibliographic data
are available on the Internet at http://dnb.d-nb.de

ISBN   978-3-8487-3566-2 (Print)
        978-3-8452-7929-9 (ePDF)

British Library Cataloguing-in-Publication Data
A catalogue record for this book is available from the British Library.

ISBN   978-3-8487-3566-2 (Print)
        978-3-8452-7929-9 (ePDF)

Library of Congress Cataloging-in-Publication Data
Marhold, Hartmut
Europe under Stress
Internal and External Challenges for the EU and its Member States
Hartmut Marhold (ed.)
165 p.
Includes bibliographic references.

ISBN   978-3-8487-3566-2 (Print)
        978-3-8452-7929-9 (ePDF)

2nd, Enlarged Edition 2017
© Nomos Verlagsgesellschaft, Baden-Baden, Germany 2017. Printed and bound in Germany.

Preface

The European Union faces multiple challenges, in these years – internal and external, economic, societal and political ones. Member states take sometimes divergent stances, vis-à-vis these common challenges, so that the EU has difficulties to emerge as the level where the solution is to be found and agreed upon.

For the last seven years or so, the financial and economic crisis has been the focus of EU policies, of efforts to withstand the pressure of financial markets, of measures to control the "sovereign" debt crisis; new instruments have been created, new institutions put in place, new forms of economic governance launched to this purpose. The crisis, however, has not yet been overcome definitely.

In the meantime, fissures in the phalanx of member states have occurred, which constitute a threat of its own for European integration: The equilibrium between France and Germany, which is an essential precondition for Europe's problem solving capacity, has been destabilised due to French problems with innovation, modernisation and competitiveness, and has lead to a mentality of defiance in France, which allows for a dangerous advance of the extreme right wing party "Front National". At both geographical ends, EU member states were or still are about to leave the Union – "exit" has become a common term, be it with regard to Greece ("Grexit") or the United Kingdom ("Brexit"). And others, like Hungary, seem to foreclose the consensus on what democracy means in Europe and to Europeans.

As if the potential for disintegration triggered by the financial and economic crisis was not enough, external challenges add to the critical agenda of the European Union, to the East and to the South. Whereas it was taken for granted, since the end of the Cold War, that the countries East of Europe would go for a smooth partnership with the EU, and that the EU would be considered as the model to follow, the conflict with Russia over the destiny of Ukraine broke out as a very bad surprise to the Europeans and endangered peace not only in Ukraine itself. Under these conditions, the fundamental question of the nature of international relations conducted by the EU, and finally the question of what sort of political system the EU would be – imperial, soft power? …, – gained unexpected attention. And this new uncertainty affects well-established partnerships, like the transatlantic relation with the United States, too.

Last not least, Europe has to rethink its engagement in global affairs on the whole, and its Mediterranean and development policy in particular. The current refugee and immigration crisis does not come as a surprise, in the long run – the destabilisation of the political regimes, and indeed the doubts over the adequacy of the Western model of the nation state for African and in particular Arab societies have been under way for a long time.

CIFE has launched a common reflection on such topics among the members of its own research team as well as colleagues and guests from various European countries. Every two weeks, one policy paper, addressing a topical issue for European integration, is being published online, since autumn 2014 – with some breaks at Christmas and during the summer, this series sums up to twenty papers, over a year. We present in this book the firs year of this series. It is not meant to give a systematic overview, but a close insight in the various, interconnected, contemporary challenges facing Europe in our time – to the point, backed by scientific expertise and underlying research, but readable for everyone who wants to get a clearer picture of central issues, crucial for Europe today.

Hartmut Marhold, Autumn 2015

Inhalt

EU internal policies and institutions

« Federalism still matters »

Perspectives fédéralistes dans le débat actuel sur la réforme de l'Union européenne

Hartmut Marhold

Pas de répit pour l'UE.

Le Traité de Lisbonne devait jeter les bases constitutionnelles de l'Union européenne pour une période de calme, sur le plan de l'évolution institutionnelle. Giscard d'Estaing n'avait-il pas annoncé que le Traité Constitutionnel allait marquer l'Union pour un demi-siècle, comme, avant, les Traités de Rome avaient marqué les Communautés européennes pour cinq décennies? Et le Traité de Lisbonne n'est il pas le Traité Constitutionnel en substance, seulement déguisé quant à sa forme? Pourtant, le calme ne s'est pas installé dans l'Union européenne au niveau de ses fondements constitutionnels – la crise financière, économique, et des budgets étatiques, ont ébranlé la confiance à peine revenue dans le nouveau traité. La crise constitue un défi qui exige une réponse européenne, et c'est en effet au niveau européen que cette crise est combattue. Cependant, la réponse se décompose en tant de mesures, directives et traités, de façon si désorganisée, individualisée, bureaucratique, successives, que la somme de ces avancées n'est pas perceptible en tant que telle. En vérité, la déjà longue série de ces mesures constitue un approfondissement incrémental de l'Union européenne qui va au-delà du Traité de Lisbonne et le fait exploser. Il ajoute désormais deux traités internationaux (le traité MES et le « pacte fiscal ») – une dynamique à couper le souffle, qui rapproche l'Union européenne de sa finalité fédérale sans que le public s'en rende compte.

D'un débat de réforme à l'autre.

La question de savoir si la politique de réforme des dernières années a vraiment, et dans quelle mesure, contribué à fédéraliser l'Union européenne par la voie d'approfondissements successifs, mériterait une analyse en soi. Mais en parallèle s'est développé un débat qui pose cette unique question: Comment sortir l'Union européenne de la crise en la transformant en une vraie fédération ? Toutefois, ce débat s'est développé sous des auspices tout à fait différents de ceux qui ont marqué le grand débat précédent, celui qui a succédé à la réalisation de l'Union monétaire (1999) et précédé la Convention constitutionnelle (2002/2003) :

a) A l'époque, le contexte était celui d'un succès d'ordre historique, le passage à la monnaie unique : l'Euro. Cela engendrait de l'enthousiasme. Alors que maintenant, la crise, avec toutes les crispations qu'elle engendre, conduit au pessimisme et au scepticisme.

b) D'autre part, l'esprit avant-gardiste des années 2000 s'opposait clairement à la réalité décevante de la politique d'intégration de ces années. Le Traité de Nice en est le symbole lamentable. Aujourd'hui, la gestion et la maîtrise de la crise par les exécutifs prennent petit à petit le pas sur l'imagination.

c) A l'époque, presque tous les chefs d'État et de gouvernement, ministres des Affaires étrangères, Présidents de la Commission européenne (anciens et actuel), députés de grande envergure, contribuaient à ce débat par leurs propres visions d'une Europe définitivement unie. Aujourd'hui, presque toute l'énergie politique est absorbée par la politique de réforme telle qu'elle est appliquée. Il semble qu'il reste peu d'énergie disponible pour l'imagination, le débat est confus et de niveau très inégal.

d) Il y a quinze ans, dominait presque sans concurrence la vision d'une Union européenne qui allait s'apparenter à la constitutionnalisation telle que connue dans les Etats-Nations, sinon transformée en un État constitutionnel fédéral lui-même; tandis qu'aujourd'hui les forces eurosceptiques, voire hostiles à la construction européenne, se manifestent avec au moins autant de force que les avocats d'une Europe fédérale.

e) Enfin, la perspective de la réforme d'il y a quinze ans était le saut qualitatif du malheureux Traité de Nice à un document constitutionnel qui allait désormais réconcilier les citoyens avec le système politique européen. Aujourd'hui, le Traité de Lisbonne n'est pas loin en deçà du Traité constitutionnel ; il représente par conséquent un haut niveau d'intégration qui laisse peu ou pas de marge pour des sauts qualitatifs supplémentaires.

Trois voies pour arriver à des perspectives fédérales

Dans ces conditions, on peut distinguer trois voies fédéralistes dans le débat actuel sur la réforme de l'Union européenne.

a) La première part de la prémisse que l'Union monétaire existe et ne la remet pas en question. Elle constate pourtant des déficits de fonctionnement et tire les conséquences « vers le haut », c'est-à-dire vers un rééquilibrage entre le degré d'intégration élevé de l'Union monétaire et le degré d'intégration trop faible dans d'autres secteurs. Certains arrivent ainsi à des conclusions de nature fédérale, qu'ils l'appellent ainsi ou non.

b) D'autres voient dans la crise actuelle une occasion d'avancer à nouveau le projet fédéraliste classique pour la construction européenne. La crise, pour eux, n'est que le déclic d'une relance de la vieille campagne pour une Europe fédérale, les adversaires étant toujours les mêmes (i.e. les États membres prétendant à une souveraineté perçue comme obsolète). L'objectif est le même : une Union européenne capable d'agir là où les États ont démontré leur défaillances.

c) La troisième dimension du débat est peut-être la plus novatrice : si la crise actuelle est une crise du modèle néolibéral, s'il faut par conséquent repenser et restructurer la relation entre les marchés (l'économie en général) et la politique, s'il faut reconquérir l'emprise de l'économie sur la politique, à quel niveau, à quel échelon faut-il le faire? Au niveau de l'État ou au niveau européen (à défaut de le faire au niveau mondial) ? Et si la question est « l'Europe », quelle Europe faut-il créer pour qu'elle puisse imposer aux marchés la règle, la « régularisation » qui soumettrait (à nouveau ?) l'économie au service de l'homme ? En d'autres termes, est-ce la conséquence inéluctable de la critique du néolibéralisme de créer une Europe fédérale ?

L'approche néo-fonctionnaliste revisitée

L'un des auteurs qui représente la première de ces trois formules – arriver à des conclusions fédérales par voie pragmatique – est l'Espagnol José Ignacio Torreblanca, qui expose la logique impitoyable de cette pensée : « Ce qui ne va pas avec l'Europe est on ne peut plus évident : si on veut avoir une monnaie commune, il faut une union bancaire, ce qui implique qu'on se dote de mécanismes de surveillances des banques, de garanties pour des avoirs en banques, et des mécanismes pour gérer des crises. Et ceci engendre un minimum de taxation commune, ainsi que des politiques fiscales qui ne procè- dent pas par le dumping. Par conséquent, il faut une coordination des politiques économiques plus poussée et une surveillance accrue des déséquilibres qui pourraient se creuser, dans l'intérêt des pays créditeurs aussi bien que des pays débiteurs. Pour des raisons évidentes, seules des institutions investies de légitimité par les ci-toyens européens peuvent assumer toutes ces tâches, et ceci pas seulement au moment de leur élection mais en permanence, concernant toutes les décisions individuellement, qui doivent se prendre sous contrôle immédi-at. L'Euro a besoin d'une puissance exécutive et législative, et des 'checks and balances' entre les deux, plutôt que la gouvernance technocratique par comité que nous avons à présent[1] . » On voit dans cette déduction logique le cheminement successif (1) de la prémisse de l'Union monétaire, (2) passant par les conséquences sur le plan des marchés financiers, (3) les po-litiques économiques et fiscales, (4) aux institutions européennes qui (5) devraient acquérir une légitimité et une structure marquées par le principe fédéral des pouvoirs et contrepouvoirs, « des checks and balances » ; la crise de l'Union monétaire exige logiquement, par l'intermédiaire de ces mesures successives, une Union fédérale[2]. Cette approche revêt un ca-ractère (néo-)fonctionnaliste, qui procède du mécanisme de spill-over d'un secteur intégré vers d'autres, pour arriver, à la fin de la série, à l'Union politique fédérale. Cette logique néofonctionnaliste semble être pure-ment « logique », c'est-à-dire neutre par rapport à des idéologies ou con-victions, qu'elles soient fédéralistes ou anti-néolibérales.

---

1 José Ignacio Torreblanca: Europe's misgovernment. European Council on Foreign Relations, online 5. April 2013; http://ecfr.eu/content/entry/commentary_euro-pes_misgovernment; reproduit dans The Federalist, a political review, Year LV, 2013, p. 3 (Introduction du numéro sous le titre„No Time Left to Lose"; traduit de l'anglais par Hartmut Marhold).

2 C'est également l'avis de Nathalie Tocci: Imagining Post-Crisis Europe. Istituto Af-fari Internazinali: Imagining Europe No. 10 (June 2014): „The underlying logic of these proposals is quintessentially functionalist." (p. 3); http://www.iai.it/pdf/Imagi ningEurope/ImaginingEurope_10.pdf . On pourrait également citer, sous cette rubrique néo-fonctionnaliste, les deux groupes de chercheurs et politiques qui com-muniquent entre eux des deux rives du Rhin, le Groupe de Glienicke (http://www.gl ienickergruppe.de/) et le Groupe Eiffel (http://www.groupe-eiffel.eu/pour-une-com munaute-politique-de-leuro/).

Le fédéralisme, comme toujours

Ce n'est pas le cas du deuxième courant du débat visant un avenir fédéral de l'Union européenne. Il y a des fédéralistes européens décidés, et ceci depuis longtemps, qui font revivre l'idée d'une Europe fédérale et voient dans la crise actuelle l'occasion d'opposer à la désorientation générale une finalité claire pour la construction européenne. Un exemple de cette approche est la proposition d'une « loi fondamentale », lancée par des députés du Parlement européen, réunis derrière leur prédécesseur Altiero Spinelli, qui avait réussi, lors de la première période législative du Parlement européen après son élection directe, entre 1979 et 1984, à élaborer et faire voter par le Parlement une Constitution européenne. Le « Groupe Spinelli » place son projet dans une perspective évolutive, selon les procédures prévues par le Traité de Lisbonne, visant une nouvelle Convention en 2015, tout en évitant le terme de « constitution » et en le remplaçant par « loi fondamentale » – c'est ainsi que les allemands appellent leur constitution. L'objectif déclaré est un «systéme politique fédéral », et les auteurs s'expliquent sur le choix du mot : « Par fédéral, nous ne visons pas un super-État, mais une Union constitutionnelle au sein de laquelle les différents échelons de gouvernement démocratique sont coordonnés, pas subordonnés. [...] Un système démocratique plus fédéral rapprocherait l'Union et ses citoyens. »[3]

Quant aux compétences d'une Union européenne réformée, l'accent est mis sur la gouvernance économique, qui devrait confier à l'Union une marge de manœuvre beaucoup plus importante, y compris le droit de lever des taxes (qui remplaceraient les contributions des États membres). Sous l'égide d'un ministre des Finances, elle aurait la possibilité de mener des politiques anticycliques, au moins pour l'Eurozone, de communautariser des dettes et de s'endetter elle-même, etc. L'architecture institutionnelle, selon ce projet, serait définitivement transformée en un système bicaméral sur le plan législatif, tandis que la Commission assumerait les fonctions de l'exécutif, d'un vrai gouvernement. Parlement et Conseil auraient des droits égaux sur tous les plans, la majorité qualifiée s'appliquerait à (pres-

---

3 The Spinelli-Group, Bertelsmann-Stiftung: A Fundamental Law of the European Union. Gütersloh 2013. Le texte a été élaboré „sous les auspices du Groupe Spinelli", dont le Conseil d'administration comprend Elmar Brok, Dany Cohn-Bendit, Andrew Duff, Isabelle Durant, Sylvie Goulard, Roberto Gualtieri, Jo Leinen and Guy Verhofstadt".

que) toutes les politiques (sauf la politique étrangère). La Charte des droits fondamentaux serait incluse dans la « loi fondamentale » (comme elle l'était dans le Traité constitutionnel). A l'avenir, les changements de traité devraient suivre la méthode de la convention, mais les conférences inter-gouvernementales ne pourraient modifier les résultats des conventions qu'avec une majorité des trois-quarts. Comme aucun État ne peut être ob-ligé de se soumettre à des règles qui vont si loin, il faudrait introduire, au lieu des divers « opt-outs », le statut de membre associé, à négocier indivi-duellement avec les candidats respectifs.

Ce projet de Loi Fondamentale veut apparaître réaliste, réalisable, et prétend déjà montrer comment le résultat d'une fédéralisation évolutive pourrait se concevoir – le texte est un traité (ou une constitution) complet. L'autre extrême de la mouvance fédéraliste, au moins sur le plan du texte, est un « pamphlet », un « manifeste », tel que Guy Verhofstadt et Daniel Cohn-Bendit l'ont publié, sous le titre « Debout l'Europe »[4], qui oppose l'Europe fédérale d'une façon beaucoup plus polémique à la résistance des États nations, qui, selon les auteurs, constitue toujours l'obstacle principal sur la voie de la fédéralisation nécessaire de l'Europe. Dans l'une comme dans l'autre version de la vision fédéraliste de l'Europe, la prémisse reste toujours la même : il faut faire abstraction des clivages politiques (par ex-emple entre le vert de gauche Cohn-Bendit et le libéral Verhofstadt) afin d'arriver, à un niveau supérieur, au consensus sur un système politique fédéral, quitte à laisser le choix de telle ou telle orientation politique aux électeurs, une fois l'Union fédérale établie.

Le Gouvernement est la solution, pas le problème – et ce gouvernement doit être à la fois fédéral et européen

Ce n'est justement pas la prémisse partagée par ceux qui voient le problème principal dans le modèle politico-économique du néolibéralis-me. Dans son discours inaugural de 1981, Ronald Reagan a marqué d'une phrase-clé l'ère néolibérale : „Government is not the solution, government is the problem" Il semble que la crise actuelle exige le renversement de cette règle. Tandis qu'il y a trente ans, dérégulation et privatisation étaient

---

4 Guy Verhofstadt et Daniel Cohn-Bendit: Debout l'Europe ! Manifeste pour une révolution postnationale en Europe, suivi d'un entretien avec Jean Quatremer. Paris (André Versaille) 2012.

les principes généraux, aujourd'hui la politique intervient à nouveau dans les marchés (financiers surtout) et la régulation du capitalisme déchainé devient une priorité politique – il suffit de penser à l'Union bancaire ou la taxe sur les transactions financières, impensables (politiquement) il y cinq, six ans. Surtout, la France a toujours envisagé le tournant néolibéral d'un œil sceptique. On considérait cette nouvelle approche « anglosaxonne » incompatible avec la culture politique française traditionnelle qui exige et espère obtenir de l'État l'orientation, voire la planification de l'avenir, également sur le plan économique et social. La critique française de l'Union monétaire a donc toujours visé l'indépendance de la Banque centrale européenne à toute directive politique et sa soumission aux règles du Monétarisme, ce qui revient grosso modo au néolibéralisme lui-même. Par contre, il aurait fallu dès la création de l'Union monétaire un « gouvernement économique », afin d'introduire au niveau européen la contrepartie politique vis-à-vis de la gestion de la monnaie commune. Cependant, cette logique conduit – en particulier en France – à un problème : si la règle de Reagan (« le gouvernement est le problème… ») est obsolète, si la solution de la crise doit être politique, il faut que cette solution, ce gouvernement, soient européens ; l'État nation n'est plus à la hauteur de la tâche. Ceci implique un « gouvernement » européen à l'instar des États nations, et ce gouvernement ne peut être autre que fédéral. Toutefois, une fédération supranationale est presque autant incompatible avec la pensée politique française que le néolibéralisme. Comment sortir de ce dilemme?

Certains auteurs français continuent à faire des efforts destinés à marier ces deux idées antagonistes, en promouvant (à nouveau) la conception d'une « Fédération des États nations ». Ce n'est pas une surprise qu'un tel projet ait été publié au nom de la Fondation Notre Europe, de Jacques Delors, qui avait lui-même plaidé pour cette formule il y a presque quinze ans. Mais ce que Roger Godino et Fabien Verdier[5] esquissent dans leur article, cache mal les contradictions inhérentes à ce projet. Ils envisagent en effet un gouvernement investi de larges pouvoirs, mais seulement pour un petit groupe de cinq à sept États membres, avec un système présidentiel qui est néanmoins soumis à la censure par une sorte de comité nommé par les États, et basé sur une assemblée parlementaire qui ne mérite pas le nom de parlement puisqu'elle serait composée de délégués des parlements

---

5 Roger Godino, Fabien Verdier: Vers la Fédération européenne. L'Europe de la dernière chance. Notre Europe, Policy Paper, 14 février 2014, online: http://www.notre-europe.eu/media/versfederationeuropeennegodinoverdierne-ijd-fev 14.pdf?pdf=ok.

nationaux, et devrait partager son pouvoir avec un sénat composé lui aussi de représentants des États, dont le nombre de sièges par État serait calculé en fonction du PIB des États membres. Les auteurs prétendent installer ainsi une Fédération « profondément démocratique »…

A l'opposé de ce projet d'une fédéralisation par le haut (et qui n'arrive pas en bas), Michel Dévoluy[6] propose une constitutionnalisation par le bas, par une levée en masse pour une Europe fédérale, assez puissante pour s'opposer au néolibéralisme, mais au nom des citoyens et pas seulement au nom des États. Dévoluy ne nie pas qu'il y a actuellement une forte intégration qui se veut fédérale, bien qu'elle se fasse sous le respect des règles néolibérales – c'est, selon lui, un « fédéralisme tutélaire », imposé par des règles de conduite sur les marchés. Ce qu'il faudrait, par contre, serait une « planification fédératrice », avec un gouvernement investi du pouvoir de guider les marchés, l'économie, les sociétés européennes, en toute indépendance des soi-disant contraintes du marché.

Quels que soient les mérites de ces réflexions, la question reste posée : ne faut-il pas une forme ou une autre de fédéralisme pour sortir l'Europe de la crise? Qu'il s'agisse de stabiliser de façon pragmatique le système politico-économique existant ou de faire succéder au néolibéralisme une Europe orientée vers le bien-être durable et soutenable; dans l'une comme dans l'autre perspective, on n'échappe pas à concevoir une vraie Fédération Européenne.

(published online mid-September 2014)

---

6 Michel Dévoluy: Comprendre le débat européen. Petit guide à l'usage des citoyens qui ne croient plus à l'Europe. Paris 2014.

Donald Tusk faces strong European challenges

Ryszard Piasecki

The enlargement of the EU was of vital significance for Poland and other Central European countries (which does not mean it was neutral or negative for the Union - quite the contrary.) For these countries, rejoining Europe was a unique opportunity for social progression, bringing the prospect of long-term benefits. If the Central European countries had not joined Europe, they would by now have been marginalized even further, with all the negative political, economic and social consequences not just for them, but for the entire European continent. Without that membership, some of the candidate countries (including Poland) could have faced many more difficulties in confronting the challenges of the technological revolution and – increasingly global - competition. Politically, if Poland were to be squeezed between the (not enlarged) EU and Russia, its sovereignty and economy would be in serious jeopardy. Refusing or not being able to join Europe would have meant that Poland would have been left permanently on the periphery of Europe. Today' s conflict between Russia and Ukraine proves that this line of reasoning was absolutely correct.

It was a unique possibility for Poland to modernize its economy as well as its social patterns, to alter ways of thinking and to enhance the social development, like the introduction of better ecological norms, better protection of consumers, higher quality of goods. However, significant progress achieved in all these domains, thanks to the EU support, did not protect Poland and other new member countries, to a lesser or greater extent, from all the consequences of the all-European crisis of today. Surprisingly, though many Poles do not accept the social inequalities and the marginalization of its 30-40% of citizens associated with the introduction of liberal economic model, only a few of them reject the integration with the European Union.

We should bear in mind that the Europe of today happens to be a very different place to what it was some 60 years ago when the EU founding members were slowly making their first steps on the road towards European integration. West European countries had plenty of time to adapt politically, economically, socially and even mentally to the challenges of working together. Unlike "new" member countries which, once admitted to the EU after queuing almost 15 years in its antechamber, had no time to waste, nor had the chance to go through the evolutionary process of European consciousness-building. They had to catch-up.

When Poland joined the European Union, the old members feared it would be as terrorizing as Spain and Greece, as arrogant as France, as complicated as Italy, and as keen on opt-outs as the United Kingdom. Ten years later and they are more likely to come asking for advice. Helped by large amounts of EU funds, Poland has become an economic and political role model for the rest of the club, growing by almost 50% over the decade and largely avoiding the lapses into populism or authoritarianism of some of the others. So it is understandable that Donald Tusk, who oversaw much of Poland's progress as prime minister between 2007 and 2014, became the first politician from "new Europe" to move into one of the EU's top positions. As president of the European Council, where Europe's heads of government meet, it falls to Mr Donald Tusk to craft deals between 28 disputatious leaders.

Crisis in the euro zone, the dangerous conflict between Russia and Ukraine and the latest terrorist threats, have reignited discussions on the adequacy of the European integration model today as well as its capacity to confront serious challenges. In particular – how to revive, still valid, European values while sorting out the economic quagmire. And how to ensure a vision of the future under the pressure of short term difficulties while averting an understandable yet unfounded loss of trust in the future of the European endeavour among the elites and parts of the populace in the – mainly older - member countries. And how to prevent disillusionment in the new EU member states, still very supportive of European integration. Last but not least, how to enhance Europe's competitiveness and position, politically and economically, on the global scene in the post-American, or post-Western world, with its uncertainty and rapid change.

This heavy challenge to European solidarity shows that EU has arrived at the cross-roads: towards renaissance – or bankruptcy. Will, however, a weakening of Europe be in the interests of either the West, with its civil standards of democracy, human rights and free markets, or indeed the world as a whole? A strong united Europe is needed to maintain a sound balance on the world scene. Amid growing interdependence under globalization, avoiding a destructive rivalry among main country groups is a precondition of a peaceful future and the wellbeing of the planet. And the mutual solving of global problems encountered. A rejuvenated Europe should take responsibility towards its citizens and the international society by deepening integration and reaffirming its values which brought, and keep, European nations together, and strengthen the European identity.

Poland is near the heart of many of the challenges facing the EU, from restarting growth to the Russian threat in Ukraine to the British problem. Some of this is circumstantial: Ukraine is Poland's neighbour, Britain the top destination for its migrant workers (more than 1 million). In the early days Polish diplomacy was defensive, concerned with voting rights or the opening of foreign labour markets. That approach persists in occasional "zero-sum" distributional debates, such as those over the EU budget or climate-change policy, that tend to reinforce Europe's old east-west split. In both cases the Poles won reasonable deals, expanding the budget and gaining exemptions from climate rules.

Elsewhere the Poles have become skilled at wrapping diplomatic initiatives in European colours. The eastern partnership, an (ultimately doomed) attempt to bring the EU's eastern neighbours, such as Ukraine, into Europe's orbit without offering them membership, was the product of an odd but fruitful alliance between Poland and Sweden. Poland has learned to move between different groupings on different issues. The "Visegrad" club (Poland, the Czech Republic, Hungary and Slovakia) is hopelessly split on Russia but united on the need for more cash from Brussels. The "Weimar triangle" (France, Germany and Poland) brings the Poles into the orbit of the EU's traditional powerhouses, even if it is more symbolic than substantial. The relationship with Germany is particularly strong, and rests on two pillars: a shared dedication to fiscal stewardship, and the business ties that have turned Polish enterprises into important suppliers for German manufacturers.

Mr Tusk's predecessor, Herman Van Rompuy, served as a sort of therapist to the EU's leaders, listening to their concerns and finding common ground where it was available, particularly on economic matters. A different approach may be expected from Mr Tusk, who elbowed his way to the top of Polish politics, sometimes ruthlessly. When appropriate he is likely to make his own views clear, especially on foreign affairs. As a veteran of the anti-communist struggle he can speak authoritatively on the European aspirations of countries like Ukraine.

Poland's hardest challenges lie ahead. Since 2004 the country has banked the easy economic and political wins, spending EU cash on infrastructure projects and reaping the diplomatic fruits of accession. It must now find a new development model based on innovation rather than cheap labour, particularly as the EU money supply dries up. And as the euro zone integrates, the longer Poland hangs on to the national currency, the further it may drift from the policy-making core. This is a concern for ministers, for among Polish voters the euro lacks friends. Two years ago nobody expected the bloody war between aggressive Russia and pro-European Ukraine. We should not forget about the new dimension of the so-called islamist terrorism that has already threatened the societies of the UK, Spain, France, Belgium and Denmark.

As for Mr Tusk, his appointment tells a story not only about Poland but about the EU. He supports the euro but has struggled to win over voters. Despite Poland staying outside, he will chair euro group summits as well as European Councils, which will please those worried by the EU's divide between euro ins and outs. He also understands the Russian threat well. Indeed, it was the Ukraine crisis that persuaded him to take the job; just days before the decision in August he was thinking of abandoning his Civic Platform party a year before an election. Yet for all that, Mr Tusk's tools will be the multilateral ones of a committed European. In particular, he hopes that his "energy union" plan will weaken Russia's ability to play divide and rule among its European customers by creating a single buyer for Gazprom's supplies. The proposal was a Polish one but would resound to Europe's advantage.

The spirit of the European solidarity is now seriously weakened, not only due to the economic crisis, but especially by the Russia- Ukraine war. To succeed, it will be essential for people of the Old Continent to become aware that it is up to them to make a crucial choice. They need to be persuaded that they bear a moral responsibility to support the right option and indicate their preference for such policies to their governments. Therefore, the time seems ripe for Europe (Europeans, heads of EU states/governments) to wake up from their dangerous lethargy, to abandon a bazaar mentality and make up their mind as to the right way forward: loose integration, i.e. going backward towards an eventual multidimensional breakup and collapse of the European Project, or the tightening of integration with a view not to aim at the superstate but, eventually, a federation that will ensure the Renaissance and reinvention of Europe, to make it ready to confront the challenges of the XXI century.

As long as the politicians and societies of member states have short memories and lack imagination, the prospect of the EU being marginalised would appear to have little impact. Should we wait for another large crisis to strike, or any external or internal threat to materialize before we agree –

and act ? The new presidency of Mr Donald Tusk could be an important point of departure towards new and fresh European thinking. It is not enough to hope for a good outcome, i.e. consolidation of the Union and regaining its solidarity, now in serious jeopardy. To avert a much worse scenario, an urgent joint educational effort has to be made to stop an increasing social indifference towards the grand and unique European Project. I strongly believe that a unified Europe and its solidarity do – in fact – serve the national interests of the EU member-states. It should continue. Lasting peace, the preservation of democracy within and among them, freedom of movement, of production factors and people and novel ideas, will greatly help - as it used to in the past – to enhance economic benefits, diminish unemployment and improve welfare throughout the European Union, with a positive impact globally as well. To this end, we need in the Union another "approfondissement": more solidarity among member-states as the basis for further integration, also in political, economic and social terms. There is also a much-neglected need to make the people of the Old Continent feel Europeans as well as being Poles, Germans or Portuguese. Let the dramatic Maidan's example - of Ukrainians determined to join Europe – awaken dormant European patriotism. Without a strengthened and united EU, we can expect the worst — militarily and politically. The history of our continent looks like repeating itself as a tragic farce in the XXI century. Frightening memories of the consequences of European nationalism 100 years ago, when the World War I started, seem to be revived eastward of Poland. An outstanding expert on the war, professor Margaret MacMillan warns that the circumstances seem to resemble those preceding that tragic event. This unwelcome and unsolicited challenge must not be ignored or underestimated by our European family.

(published online end of February 2015)

How neo-liberal is the EU crisis policy?

Hartmut Marhold

The crisis policy of the EU has often been characterised as following a neo-liberal path[1] and has, for this reason, been widely criticised. Is this justified? Some doubts may arise when a wholly different criticism, no less often put forward, is taken into account: the EU does not follow any path at all, but improvises without knowing where it's going. Isn't there any coherence, then, in the way in which the EU tries to overcome (if not solve) the crisis?

The whole confusing programme ... One banal answer is that things are not simple or easy anyway, and we would not come to a convincing conclusion without a differentiating look into the various instruments the EU has developed and put into force over the years since the outbreak of the crisis in 2008. These instruments are of a very different nature indeed – from pure promises among the heads of state and government (so-called "pacts", as, for eg., the "Euro-Plus-Pact") about policies within the framework of the existing structures (like the investment programmes in 2008/09 and 2014/15), dozens of regulations and directives (like the "Six-Pack", and "Two-Pack"-Regulations), switches in the decision making procedures (like the reversed Qualified Majority in the case of fines, to the advantage of the Commission) to new agencies and institutions (like the various new bureaucracies in the "European System of Financial Supervision", ESFS, and the Banking Union) and genuinely new international treaties (like the "European Security Mechanism", ESM, with its own institutional setting, and the "Fiscal Pact", with its strange use of the EU in-

---

1 To make it very short, for the sake of this format, let us suppose that the Washington Compromise is still the reference for what may be described as neo-liberal, despite so much differentiation; and that means to reduce the role of government, to withdraw the state from economic intervention, to shrink public budgets in favour of private economic actors, to privatise not only state held economic assets, but public services, to deregulate markets, to impose the rules of market conform behaviour even on the state, etc.

stitutions). Is there any logical, coherent, or even theory based structure in these instruments, beyond this formal (and incomplete) classification?

Four categories of crisis policy instruments. We might distinguish four types of measures, with regard to their political aims and intentions: (1) First, there was and is again something like an interventionist policy, mobilising and allocating huge funds in order to prevent the economy from melting down. The European Economic Recovery Programme, launched in 2008, was the first one, the 315 billion € programme of the Juncker-Commission is a second attempt of a similar kind. (2) A second category of instruments consists of rescue funds, designed to prevent Eurozone member states from bankruptcy. The "European Financial Security Facility" (EFSF) and the ESM are part of this group, but so is the European Central Bank's OMT programme. (3) The third set of measures concerns the control of member states´ compliance with the pre-established rules of behaviour in the Eurozone – the "European Semester", Six-Pack, Two-Pack, Euro-Plus-Pact, Fiscal Pact are all part of this group. (4) Finally, there are a number of instruments aimed at regulating the financial market, at least in Europe, binding the actors on this market to rules and controlling them; the above mentioned ESFS (not to be confused with EFSF!), the Banking Union, and Financial Transaction Tax (and their complex internal structures) are of this kind. If we have a look at each of these groups of political instruments to cope with the crisis, and ask ourselves how neo-liberal they are, our findings should furnish us with an overall answer to the initial question.

(1) Economic Recovery and Investment Programmes. The "European Economic Recovery" Plan of 2008/09 was an emergency rescue programme, launched hastily by the heads of state and government, when they became aware that their first hope – that the crisis would be restricted to the USA and the financial sector – proved to be an illusion. Germany alone increased its public debt by approximately 20%, under this pressure, from 60 to 80% of its GDP. The EU member states on the whole spent something like 1,5 billion € in order to prevent the worst, in the financial sector and the "real" economy. Concrete measures varied from one country to the other – incentives for buying new cars in Germany, cheap loans for SMEs in France, the aim was the same everywhere: a massive increase in purchasing power and "intelligent investment", state driven. There cannot be any doubt that such a strategy is classical Keynesianism, just the opposite of what neo-liberal theory would require, regardless of the theoretical consciousness of the actors, regardless of whether the strategy is

sustainable or not. We only have to state that the first, and very substantial reaction to the crisis was not a neo-liberal one, but Keynesian. The second attempt of a similar kind, the investment programme launched by the Juncker-Commission (and, more precisely, by Jean-Claude Juncker himself), is slightly different in terms, but not very far from the strategic approach. It is different in so far as the 315 billion € Juncker promises to mobilise are not entirely drawn from public budgets, on the contrary: 21 billion only should come directly from the tax-payers (and some say that they did already pay, since these 21 billion are already part of the convened-upon EU budget, over the next three years), used as a leverage to mobilise up to fifteen times this sum in terms of private investment – a hope, or promise, for the time being. And – the second difference in comparison to 2008/09 – the programme is not driven by the panic that everything might melt down, but by the analysis that after years of austerity, of shrinking budgets and state activity, there must be a re-launch of investment, initiating new growth. The overall approach, however, stays the same: It is a political task to take care of investment, growth, allocation of resources, a political task now to be taken up at the European level, no longer exclusively by the member states – Keynesian still, just as six years ago. But it is a one (or two) shot policy, not a deliberate long-term strategy.

(2) Rescue funds. Not quite as easy is the qualification of the rescue funds, destined to save Eurozone member states from becoming victims of speculation, i.e. saving them from the evil impacts of financial markets. ESFS, with its 780 billion € guarantees (and 440 billion € credit lines), ESM (with its 702 billion €) and the ECB's OMT (Outright Monetary Transactions) programme (nothing more, for the time being, than a promise to save the € in any event, by buying member states´ bonds without limits, if needed) – all three of them protect states against markets, withdraw states from the rules of markets, instead of submitting them to these rules and enforcing them on states themselves, obliging them to act as if they were economic actors. For this reason, all the three instruments and are anything but neo-liberal. But if we consider the conditions under which the funds are handed out to the states in distress (Greece in particular, since Spain, Portugal and Ireland did already escape from their financial assistance programmes), we must state that the "conditionality" between European credits and structural reforms required from the assisted countries introduces a large share of neo-liberal policies. The counterpart of financial assistance is in most cases a severe cut in public spending, a

reduction of public services, of social assistance - in short, a shrinking of the welfare state for the sake of and to the benefit of economic competitiveness. The so-called Fiscal Compact, an international treaty on its own, obliging the member countries to introduce the rule of (nearly) balanced budgets at a constitutional level, in the hierarchy of their law system, is not much more than an attempt to make these principles respected. The huge rescue funds (around 140 billion € for Greece, over time, i.e. approximately the equivalent of one whole annual EU budget) are all more or less instruments to enforce neo-liberalism in the "benefiting" countries. This side of the affair is even reinforced by the implication of the IMF in these programmes (if the IMF can still be regarded as the guardian of the temples of neo-liberalism).

(3) Supervision, control and enforcement of macroeconomic rules. The third group in the arsenal of crisis combat is a series of rules and regulations, bound together by the concern to improve the enforcement of the requirements for membership in the Monetary Union, originally enshrined in the Maastricht Treaty, consolidated in the Stability and Growth Pact, itself adapted and modified in 2005. The crisis obliged many Eurozone member states (Germany included, see above) to expand their public debt far beyond the allowed 60 % of the GDP. In some cases, like Germany, investors on the financial markets never had doubts about the reliability of the debtors; others were not so happy and speculated on their potential failure. Protection against this speculation triggered on the one hand the solidarity expressed in the previous group of measures, i.e. financial rescue funds; on the other hand, the luckier member states now insisted on the criteria for membership in the Eurozone being strictly respected. The operational criteria for membership, based on the Stability and Growth Pact, were tightened, control increased and made nearly permanent with several deadlines over the year, the menace of fines made more credible, the conditionality between respect of the criteria and structural reforms enlarged to nearly all fields of macroeconomic policy, by means of "country specific recommendations". These recommendations were narrowed down to detailed policy recommendations like reducing public spending for pensions, further deregulating the labour market, cutting down the public sector etc. And the Commission was entitled to impose fines, should these rules not be respected, except where there was a qualified majority of member states against this punishment – a decisive reversal of the decision making rules between Commission and Council, to the benefit of the former; previously, the positive qualified majority in the Council was re-

quirèd to pass the Commission proposals. These new rules were enshrined in the European Semester, which establishes the rhythm for control, the so-called Six-Pack (five regulations and one directive) and another Two-Pack (two more regulations), as well as the Euro-Plus-Pact, a voluntary commitment of the Eurozone, plus five or six other EU members, going even beyond the requirements of the legal framework. There can be no doubt that this group of measures is inspired by a neo-liberal approach, fully in line with the Stability and Growth Pact, itself dating back to the peak of the neo-liberal era and paradigm. It does not come as a surprise, under these conditions, that a President of the French Republic is at odds with the Commission when told that he has to pass this or that law in order to deregulate labour markets and cut down health care expenditure …

(4) Regulating the financial market. A widely different approach is characteristic for the last group of instruments to combat the crisis: Financial market regulation. It soon became clear in the eyes of the heads of state and government, European Commission and Parliament that there had to be a U-turn with regard to regulation on the financial markets, after the outbreak of the crisis. The ambitions went very far, the often repeated formula was that "no actor, no product, no sector, no territory should any longer be able to escape sensible and intelligent regulation and supervision", as Commissioner Michel Barnier put it in 2010 (http://www.cnbc.-com/id/39023082#.; Angela Merkel used the same words). Even if the reality, in 2015, is far from this goal, the Commission launched an avalanche of legal acts (forty or so, they say) in order to cover most of the products, sectors, and territories. Whatever the extent of this wave of regulation may be or may become in the future, the change of paradigm is remarkable: up to then, no other economic sector was such a privileged model pupil of neo-liberal politics as the financial markets – and now this market was overrun by regulation. Three instruments in particular are of outstanding importance: The ESFS – the European System of Financial Supervision -, the Banking Union and the Financial Transaction Tax. ESFS, as the title indicates, is not a single instrument, but a whole system, a set of agencies, entitled to supervise and regulate banks and insurance companies, securities, stocks and bonds. However, these agencies, created between 2009 and 2011, proved to be still too far away from concrete action on the markets – as the Cyprus banking crisis made crucially obvious. Plans to establish a fully fledged Banking Union came into play and were indeed implemented in 2014, with a mandate for the ECB to control nearly every step of the 130 or so most important banks in Europe (in close coop-

eration with national authorities, to submit to common rules, when controlling the rest of the 6000 European financial actors). The Banking Union comprises three main institutional pillars: (1) the SSM (Single Supervisory Mechanism), charged with the enforcement and control of stricter rules (concerning e.g. the mandatory increase of equity capital), (2) the SRM (Single Resolution Mechanism), created to liquidate banks when failing, instead of feeding them with tax payers´money (and the liquidation should be paid now by the shareholders/owners first, by a common fund of 55 billion €, supplied by the banks themselves, and by public money only as the last option); (3) a DGS (Deposit Guarantee Scheme), a mechanism to protect consumers from losing their money when a bank fails. Despite all criticism vis-à-vis this construction and its weaknesses (the resolution fund seems to be small in comparison with the risks etc.), the Banking Union as such can hardly be overestimated as a political move away from free financial markets; some people (as Andreas Dombret, Director of the German Bundesbank) went so far as to regard the Banking Union as the most important step to European Integration since Monetary Union – more important than the Nice or Lisbon Treaties. Finally, some member states got an attempt to tax financial transactions under way – less than half of the Eurozone members, for some financial products only, and with very low taxes, but nevertheless breaking a (neo-liberal) taboo. On the whole, the more than thirty European laws which are in force today, regulating the financial markets, are probably the most evident step away from a purely neo-liberal approach to this sector of the economy. However, they are not supposed to substitute themselves for the market as such, on the contrary: their purpose is to make markets function again. The shift, or U-turn, in the approach lies with the conviction that markets need to be regulated to be functional – not deregulated. The setting is classical ordo-liberalism, following theories, models and politics of the German (mainly Freiburg) branch of what was called, for a short time after WWII, neo-liberalism, but soon diverged profoundly into the Anglo-Saxon (and Austrian) School (Hayek, Friedman and their followers) on the one hand, and the "Social Market Economy" (or Rhine or Rhenish Capitalism) on the European Continent.

Conclusions. The whole picture of the EU crisis policy is multi-faceted. It cannot be reduced to a simple enforcement of neo-liberal rules on countries which tried to escape from the painful adaptation to international competitiveness. Some very important measures comply with Keynesian theory, as e.g. the huge sums injected into the purchasing power of the people, or in businesses and companies. Others seem to come straight out of the neo-liberal toolbox, like the recommendations to deregulate labour markets and cut public spending for social security, aiming indeed at increasing international competitiveness at the expense of the middle-class (or inferior social stratum). Others still tend to politically organise and guarantee, regulate and supervise the functioning of (financial) markets. The variety of measures and instruments may be seen either as a series of confused, incoherent political actions, without guidelines and even less theoretical foundation – or as a remarkably rich policy mix, free from any ideology (neo-liberal or otherwise), and adapted to a particularly complex challenge. One thing, however, is sure: The winner of the game is the European Union, the European level of governance. When Ronald Reagan, in his inaugural address in 1981, spelled out the neo-liberal credo – "Government is not the solution, government is the problem" –, he was thinking of government at the level of the (American) federal state, of course; the current crisis, in contrast, has contributed towards shifting much of "government" to the European level. And (European) government is no longer considered to be the problem, it is supposed to bring about the solution again. The crisis did change not only the underlying economic theory, but the European multilevel governance system, too, in favour of a stronger Europe.

(published online mid-January 2015)

Le défi de l'harmonisation fiscale en Europe

Jean-Claude Vérez

La question de l'harmonisation fiscale (assimilée à une égalisation des taux d'imposition et/ou à une uniformité de l'assiette fiscale) ou de la concurrence fiscale en Europe n'est pas récente. Si les avis sont partagés quant au bienfait de la première, on admettra que les contraintes du traité de Maastricht puis du Pacte de stabilité et de croissance signifiaient que les États se devaient de réduire leurs dépenses et/ou d'accroître leurs recettes afin de stopper leur niveau d'endettement. En période de croissance, les recettes fiscales à taux de fiscalité inchangé augmentent. En période de crise, ce n'est plus le cas de sorte que les politiques menées par les uns ou par les autres peuvent diverger. Or, toute réforme fiscale au niveau de l'UE peut avoir des effets pervers si elle est menée de manière désordonnée. Elle peut notamment déboucher sur une concurrence entre les pays : les uns, dans un souci de reprise économique, cherchent à attirer les investisseurs via une baisse de leur fiscalité pendant que les autres, contraints par la crise, élèvent leurs taux d'imposition pour limiter les déficits, conformément à leurs engagements européens.

Il y a plus de quinze ans, le Cepii (2000) alertait déjà les autorités en précisant que dans un tel contexte de concurrence fiscale, l'harmonisation fiscale européenne représentait « une source importante de tensions entre les pays européens, en particulier pour ce qui concerne la fiscalité du capital, facteur rendu de plus en plus mobile avec la disparition du risque de change à l'intérieur de la zone euro ». En l'absence de coopération européenne, outre le fait que des États peuvent chercher à attirer des entreprises en réduisant le taux et/ou l'assiette de l'impôt, certains peuvent aller plus loin en adoptant des régimes discriminatoires favorables aux entreprises étrangères à tel point que le pas est vite franchi pour dépasser le stade de la concurrence (fiscale) et pratiquer in fine du dumping (fiscal). Pour y parvenir, l'État réduit « le taux d'imposition de manière drastique, pour attirer les contribuables. L'Irlande, qui impose à 10 % seulement les bénéfices des entreprises multinationales (en principe jusqu'au 31 décembre 2010), est ainsi souvent suspectée de dumping ».

L'harmonisation fiscale, à l'opposé de ce type de pratique qui repose sur des intérêts strictement nationaux, exige « une solution négociée dont le but est d'encadrer les taux et les assiettes, pour éviter les distorsions fiscales et le basculement de la charge de l'impôt sur les assiettes les moins mobiles ».

Au cours de ces quinze dernières années, la situation en Europe est restée contrastée et pour cause : outre les avis divergents entre l'UE à 28 sur la « bonne » politique fiscale à mener, les mesures exigent un accord à l'unanimité conformément à l'article 223.2 du Traité sur le fonctionnement de l'UE alors que les disparités sont nombreuses. En 2012, les recettes fiscales dans l'Union européenne ont atteint 39,4 % du PIB. L'impôt sur le travail reste la principale source de recettes fiscales. Rapportées au PIB de l'État, les charges fiscales (en incluant les contributions sociales) ont varié en 2012 de moins de 30 % en Lituanie et en Irlande à 45 % en France et 48 % au Danemark (www.touteleurope.eu.).

On relève également des différences européennes en ce qui concerne le taux maximum d'imposition sur le revenu avec un clivage entre l'Europe de l'Ouest et l'Europe de l'Est : le taux oscille de 10 % en Bulgarie, à 15 % en Lituanie…et à près de 57 % en Suède. La France se situe dans la moyenne de l'Europe occidentale.

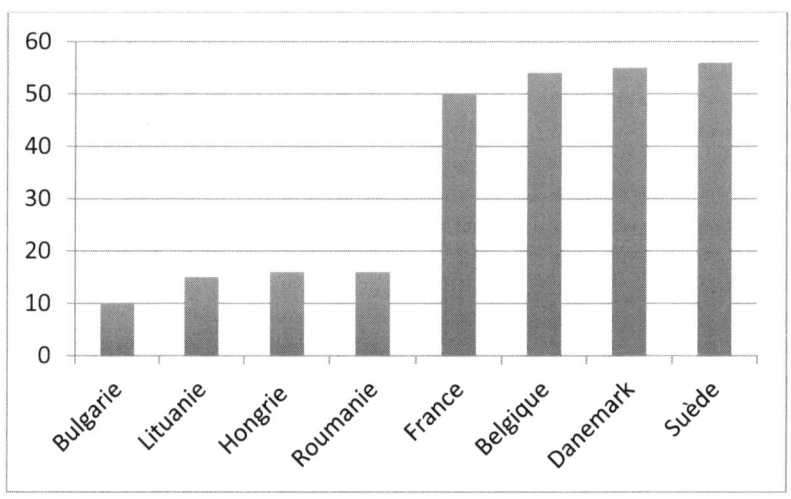

Concernant les taux normaux de TVA, les écarts sont nettement moins importants. Ils vont de 15 % au Luxembourg à 19 % en Allemagne et à 27 % en Hongrie.

Cela tient en partie au marché unique difficilement compatible avec des taxes indirectes trop disparates. En revanche, en matière d'impôt sur les sociétés, on constate de nouveau des écarts avec en 2013, un taux maximal d'imposition pour les entreprises à 10 % en Bulgarie contre 36,1 % en France.

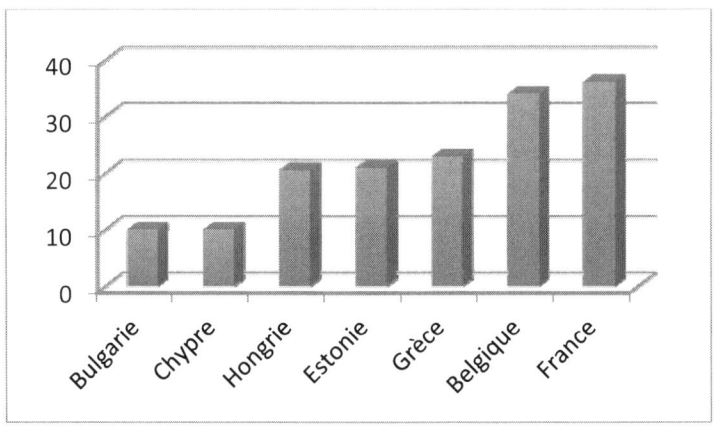

Figure 2 : Taux d'imposition sur les sociétés / Eurostat 2014

Selon la note 14 du CAE (juillet 2014), il convient de « plaider pour davantage d'harmonisation fiscale en Europe essentiellement du fait que la concurrence fiscale nuit au bon fonctionnement du marché unique. Par ailleurs, la crise de la zone euro a fait émerger un débat sur la nécessité de compléter la monnaie unique avec une « capacité budgétaire », ce qui soulève immédiatement la question des ressources, et donc de la coopération fiscale. Enfin, les modèles de concurrence fiscale établissent une distinction entre les « petits » pays (qui considèrent les variables internationales comme des données exogènes) et les « grands » pays (qui ont un impact sur l'économie mondiale). L'un des enjeux de la coordination/ coopération dans l'Union européenne est de faire bénéficier l'ensemble des « petits pays » européens de la force d'un « grand pays », avec une plus grande maîtrise collective de la politique fiscale » (p.9).

Au-delà de la dimension économique de notre interrogation, il y a bien entendu un questionnement politique qui peut laisser penser que la coopération fiscale puis l'harmonisation fiscale constitue une des étapes préalables à l'union politique. Les défenseurs de la concurrence fiscale ne s'y trompent pas : la souveraineté des Nations permet de délimiter le champ de l'espace social, le niveau de redistribution des revenus et de facto le niveau des prélèvements. C'est encore le moyen d'opérer une limite entre biens privés et biens publics dès lors que ces derniers exigent des financements. Toute politique fiscale harmonisée ou unique qui se substituerait à la concurrence fiscale constituerait donc une atteinte à la souveraineté nationale.

À l'opposé, les détracteurs de la concurrence ou du dumping fiscal (à ne pas confondre), dénoncent une Europe à plusieurs vitesses avec à la clé des comportements d'optimisation fiscale, d'évasion fiscale incompatibles avec le projet européen. Du fait de la mondialisation et du basculement du monde qui voit une partie substantielle de l'Asie se hisser aux premiers rangs des grandes puissances, l'Europe a tout à perdre si elle accentue la concurrence en son sein plutôt que de se hisser en bloc face à la concurrence extérieure.

La note du CAE en veut pour preuve la décision récente de l'Union bancaire en complément de l'Union monétaire. En quoi cette Union bancaire est-elle compatible avec des taux d'imposition différenciés entre l'UE-28 ? « Il est nécessaire d'éliminer les distorsions liées aux impôts au sein de l'union bancaire puisque celles-ci ne sont pas cohérentes avec le principe de régulation et de contrôle uniques des banques. Deuxièmement, les distorsions existantes entre les banques et le secteur non financier doivent être éliminées et une imposition commune permettrait d'atteindre cet objectif, en complément d'une régulation adaptée à chacun des deux secteurs » (p.10).

Enfin, il est vraisemblable qu'une politique fiscale convergente qui pourrait précéder une harmonisation fiscale soit de nature à amener l'Europe vers une Union budgétaire. On sait que toute politique économique repose a minima sur trois instruments : monétaire, budgétaire, fiscal. On peut y associer des objectifs de politique industrielle, de politique sociale, de politique environnementale, etc. Mais personne ne doute un seul instant que la politique économique d'un pays ou d'un bloc régional comme l'UE exige des recettes pour financer les dépenses. De fait, les instruments budgétaires et fiscaux sont étroitement liés.

Pour autant, rien ne doit laisser penser qu'une harmonisation fiscale européenne et, demain (?) une union budgétaire, aient comme objectif prioritaire une hausse des prélèvements et des dépenses de la zone. C'est plutôt le contraire qui est à l'œuvre avec la règle d'or et le Mécanisme européen de stabilité (MES). Du reste, eu égard au niveau de prélè- vements fiscaux en vogue dans le reste du monde, il apparaît plus sage de resserrer les écarts plutôt que de les accentuer, conscients que cette stratégie pose inéluctablement la question du financement de la protection sociale au sein de l'Europe.

La coordination des politiques fiscales (voire l'harmonisation fiscale) apparaît comme une solution efficace mais le chemin est et sera long ; pour des raisons économiques et politiques, c'est un processus lent mais, de notre point de vue, inéluctable pour asseoir encore et toujours plus la cohésion européenne.

Références

CEPII, 2000, L'économie mondiale 2001, La Découverte, Repères.
CAE, 2014, « Renforcer l'harmonisation fiscale en Europe », n° 14, juillet.
Merci à Laurent Baechler pour ses remarques et suggestions pertinentes.

(published online end of January 2015)

The Juncker-Plan - a New Paradigm?

Hartmut Marhold

Europe needs investment.

To come out of the crisis, Europe needs not only sound public finances – Europe needs economic growth, too. Growth provides the basis for both jobs and taxes income (i.e. sound budgets) alike. And growth will not return to Europe without a huge wave of investment. That is what the Juncker-Plan is all about: mobilising 315 billion € for investment in Europe, over the next three years, in order to initiate long term economic growth, thereby reducing unemployment and creating the conditions for taxes being paid. The growth rates, for 2015, will be around zero. In some states of the Eurozone, the unemployment rate has reached in some states more than a quarter of the population (and more than the half of the youth), and the investment rate is 15% below what it was before the crisis, in 2007. The financial markets and the "sovereign" debt crisis may be more or less under control (though not solved), but the real economy is certainly a huge concern.

A second attempt to make the economy work.

Juncker's plan is the second attempt, since the beginning of the crisis, to make the economy work – the first one, launched in 2008, shortly after the outbreak of the crisis, intended to avoid the worst, to prevent a general melt-down of the European economy, to reduce the intensity of the unavoidable recession in the wake of the financial crisis. This first strategic move was triggered by panic, and most of the member states of the EU invested more money than they had – in fact, all of them broke the rule of limiting public debt to a maximum 60% of the GDP. Some got out of the mess, more or less successfully (Germany), due to their international competitiveness, others did not (Greece) – their debt has not only failed to shrink since then, but has engulfed them into an ever less sustainable budgetary disaster. Whatever the case, no European member state can afford such an approach for a second time.

"Leverage" is the key.

But what can be done, then, if the budgetary potential of the European nation states is exhausted and the economy does not pick up steam by itself? Jean-Claude Juncker claims to have the solution: Only 21 out of the 315 billion € should come from public budgets (European, this time, not national), whereas fifteen times this basic sum should come from private investors: "leverage" is the key. And this is the most interesting aspect of the new approach. Why should private investors provide fifteen times the amount of the public share? How should it be implemented? What does it mean for the relationship between politics and the economy?

Will it work? Nobody knows, but there has been a precedent to such an approach, e.g. at the European Investment Bank, the bank of the European Union. The EIB reached an unprecedented 1:18 leverage ratio between its own (public) capital and private investment after the increase of its capital in 2013, and even a 1:20 ratio within the framework of a programme called COSME, aimed at facilitating investment for SME's. Certainly, this was on a smaller scale – but the proof that it is not completely illusionary has been delivered by the EU's own bank itself.

No risk, only fun.

But why would private investors, by adding 15 € of their own to only 1 € of a public authority, be prepared to run into such a risk? Simply because there is no risk: The one and only public € is the guarantee that the risk for the given investment has been examined, evaluated, tested by the public authority providing the initial 1 €, and it is the public authority which ultimately takes on (what is no longer considered to be) the risk. It is then extremely attractive for private investors to put up their capital under the risk-free protection of a public authority.

Steering investment towards strategic fields ...

"Public authority", in this case, means the European Commission and the European Investment Bank. But here's where the problem starts – which of the two will really decide, which project deserves investment and which does not? Whatever the case, the choice is crucial, anyway: The European Commission launched its plan on the 26 November 2014 (and the European Council endorsed it on the 18 December), but Juncker had already outlined the shape of the plan much earlier, i.e. on the 15 July, while he was still candidate for the presidency of the Commission and not yet elected: "The focus of this additional investment should be in the areas of infrastructure, notably broadband and energy networks, as well as transport infrastructure in industrial centres; education, research and innovation; and renewable energy and energy efficiency. A significant amount should be channelled towards projects that can help the younger generation back to work"[1] (repeated and confirmed in the document of 26 November). This is a political, a strategic vision of "steering" investment towards the real economy, towards profitable projects[2].

... or attracting investment towards profitable projects?

On the other hand, these projects need to be profitable, otherwise private investors would not come in, no matter how attractive risk-free investment may be. Profitability, however, is not a political criterion, nor is it a macroeconomic or a strategic one - but a business, a microeconomic criterion. The EIB made it clear that in their eyes projects should be selected on a non-political basis, by experts and expertise, putting profitability in the forefront, with no preconceived plan for privileged regions (e.g. European states which need more investment than others) or sectors (e.g. the "strategic" ones indicated by Juncker).

---

1 http://ec.europa.eu/priorities/jobs-growth-investment/plan/- docs/an-investment-pla n-for-europe_com _2014 _903_en.pdf (15.3.2015).
2 The English version of the programme says that plan is intended to "make the investment reach" the real economy, the German version is more explicit in theoretically relevant terms – it says that investment should be "steered" (or "channelled", "directed"); the German term is "Lenkung" and that is undoubtedly "Keynesian" speech.

How is it possible to marry these fundamentally different criteria for the selection of projects? How does one decide whether a project gets funding and risk-sharing (under the umbrella of the public share in funds), when the interests in projects are based on different assumptions?

The European Fund for Strategic Investment (EFSI)

The whole 315 billion € should be channelled through a new fund, the "European Fund for Strategic Investment"[3], which will not be an in its own right, but a branch or department of the European Investment Bank. The EIB emerges as the central actor in this setting, and that is only logical: As a bank, the EIB is close to investment as private actors understand it; as a public institution, it is close to the political sphere and its "strategic" interests. But this central situation of the EFSI, within the institutional framework of the EIB, is the very focal point of a topical problem: There are heavy disputes surrounding the governance of the fund at present, which threaten to delay the launch of the investment itself, despite the efforts of Juncker to accelerate the preparation as much as possible: He wants the fund to be operational by end of June.

The EFSI governance structure: Who has the power over 315 billion €?

The governance of the EFSI is based on a three level approach, starting at the top with a "Steering Board": It „will decide on the overall orientation, the investment guidelines, the risk profile, strategic policies and asset allocation of the Fund. As long as the EIB and the Commission are the only contributors to the EFSI, the number of members and votes will be allocated based on size of their contributions and all decisions will be taken by consensus."

What comes next is an „Investment Committee": It „will be accountable to the Steering Board. It will vet specific projects and decide which will receive EFSI support, without any geographic or sectoral quotas. The

---

3 ESFI, which adds one acronym more to the already very rich range of such things, since the outbreak of the crisis – who finds his way in the jungle of ESFS, EFSF, EFSM, ESM, etc. … and now ESFI?

Committee will consist of six independent market experts and a Managing Director".

The crucial question is "how the EFSI governance structure will ensure independence from the public and private contributors? - The use of the guarantee fund for each individual investment decision will be validated by the Investment Committee consisting of independent professionals re-ceiving a remuneration for their work in compliance with the investment guidelines. These independent experts shall have a high level of relevant market experience, inter alia in project finance, and be appointed by the Steering Board for a renewable fixed term of three years."[4]

In the eyes of the President of the European Investment Bank, the Ger-man (former high ranking – liberal – diplomat) Werner Hoyer, this provi-sional structure is still far from ruling out any conflict - on the contrary: He deplores the fact that there is a power struggle going on, aiming to gain control of the way in which future investment will be steered.

Is the Juncker-Plan a new paradigm in the relationship between politics and the economy?

Juncker thinks so: "This is a Plan that will fundamentally change public policy and the financing tools underpinning investment in Europe [...] The Plan presented today is the first step in a new direction."[5] His arguments: The idea of the (see "leverage") Plan is not wholly new, but this time it is launched at an unprecedented level, and its political importance for the whole of Europe is immense. Never before has a political move aiming at economic growth been undertaken on this scale and with these methods. Juncker insists that it is totally different from the "European Investment Programme" of 2008: "This investment programme will not be a recovery plan of the kind that some Member States tried to introduce in the 1970s. Such recovery plans produce no more than a flash in the pan." If this can be seen as a refusal of any return to Keynesian policies, Juncker distances

---

4 All the three previous quotations from: European Commission: The European Fund for Strategic Investments (EFSI) Questions and Answers, http://ec.europa.eu/priorit ies/jobs-growth-investment/- plan/docs/efsi_qa_en.pdf (15.3.2015).
5 Communication from the Commission, Brussels, 26.11.2014 COM(2014) 903 final, http://ec.europa.eu/priorities/jobs-growth-investment/plan/docs/an-investment-plan-for-europe_com_2014_903 _en.pdf (15.3.2015).

himself equally from the more neo-liberal policies based on the assumption that austerity is the key to healthy conditions for growing economies: "But I also want to urge some colleagues to abandon the idea that only harsh austerity and excessive cost-cutting will automatically revive the forces for growth and stimulate the labour market. By the same token, deficits and high levels of debt do not automatically produce growth."[6] This shows equal distance to Keynes and Friedman, to Keynesianism and Neoliberalism.

The new approach does not yet have a doctrinal basis or background. It is nevertheless innovative and deserves theoretical attention. Based on the political will to have a say in where the economy evolves, in steering investment towards strategic goals, in trusting in the capacity of politics to have an impact on markets, investment, growth and jobs – and not only by setting the general conditions, but by intervening and interfering in the markets – , the Juncker approach leaves on the other hand much room for private action, does not substitute the "state" (i.e. the European Union, in this case) for markets and actors on these markets, allows for freedom to invest or not in projects, which are certified to be both strategic and profitable alike.

In Juncker's mind, his approach should spread to the whole of public budgets – a far reaching perspective, and a courageous proposal, ahead of any experience with the current plan itself. A system of investment certification should evolve on the basis of the future experience of the EFSI, a "single-entry investment advisory 'Hub'"[7] for sound investment should be established, and more and more public budgets, at the national and the European level, should be submitted to the "leverage"-rule: Politics would acquire the role of an engine, a driving force – neither a substitute for the whole train, nor simply laying down the rails and waiting for the trains to come …

(published online mid-March 2015)

---

6 Juncker's Speech at the European Parliament, 22 October 2014: Time for Action – Statement in the European Parliament plenary session ahead of the vote on the College; http://europa.eu/rapid/- press-release_SPEECH-14-1525_en.htm; the speech at YouTube: https://www.youtube.com/watch?v=XGiSrYwkm_0 (15.3.2015). He could have added that the European Recovery Plan of 2008 was still very much of the same kind ...

7 See footnote 6.

EMU: The Way Forward

Philippe Maystadt

The crisis in the euro-area, triggered by the financial crisis but fuelled by the macroeconomic imbalances that have emerged since the establishment of the single currency, has shown *the fundamental deficiency* of a design where the monetary policy is integrated while the stabilisation instruments remain at the national level. The euro-area has already adopted *significant reforms* with a view to addressing this deficiency.

First, *a safety net* was created, the so-called « European Stability Mechanism » (ESM), to provide access to finance in case of acute market-financing difficulty. It is an important addition to the European policy architecture but it does not provide support to countries still benefitting from market access[1]. The fact that the ESM can bring support only at a very late stage is reinforced by two features of the mechanism. First, its intergovernmental nature implies that some national parliaments have de facto a veto right on aid disbursements to partner countries, which means that a level of uncertainty remains. Second, the conditionality attached to ESM support appears so severe that national governments do not ask for help until in desperate need. So the ESM has no opportunity to intervene when problems are emerging.

The second significant response was *a very sizeable provisioning of liquidity* by the European Central Bank. This helped to finance banks in the south of Europe, many of which were and some still are shut out of the market. Abundant ECB liquidity has prevented a major banking crisis and has reduced funding tensions. The ECB has contributed to financial stability – which is of course a major achievement – but it could not substitute for the absence of fiscal stabilisation.

Third, *a new macroeconomic imbalance procedure* was established to detect the development of macroeconomic vulnerabilities early on and exert pressure on Member States to correct them. The so-called « *European*

---

1 See J. Pisani-Ferry, E. Vihriälä and G. Wolff : « Options for a Euro-Area Fiscal Capacity », Bruegel Policy Contribution, January 2013.

semester » allows the Commission to propose and the Council to adopt « country-specific recommendations ». These two innovations move in the right direction: Member States receive guidance on growth-enhancing structural reforms before they are discussed by national parliaments. But their impact is still limited, notably because they lack appropriate democratic legitimacy due to the modest involvement of the European Parliament and of the national parliaments.

Fourth, *the reform of the « Stability and Growth Pact »* and *the agreement on the « Fiscal Compact »* were intended to reinforce the fiscal framework in order to prevent the building up of large fiscal imbalances in the future. The introduction of *the reverse qualified majority* for decisions under both the excessive deficit procedure and the macroeconomic imbalance procedure was supposed to increase the quasi-automaticity of the sanctions. But, of course, if the Commission does not dare to propose sanctions when a big country is concerned, the effectiveness of the system is reduced.

The fifth - and in my view most significant - response was the establishment of *the Banking Union* in order to break the vicious circle connecting banks and sovereigns. A well functioning banking union will allow credit markets to act as stabilisers. However, "it is not certain that the credit channel by itself can provide enough stabilization"[2]. Moreover, the third pillar of the banking union – the joint deposit guarantee – is still missing. This third pillar would prevent disruptive capital outflows; as long as it is missing, the only possible response in case of capital flight from a country, as it was evident during the Cyprus crisis, is the reintroduction of capital controls, which violates a basic principle not only of the EMU but of the EU itself.

Even if the banking union was completed with the third pillar, would these five responses be sufficient to provide the needed stabilisation? My answer is : No. In full agreement with the Four Presidents' Report of December 2012[3], I firmly believe that further steps for the euro-area integration need to be taken. Ultimately, a monetary union that is supposed to be stable and irreversible must be also an economic union.

A preliminary remark: when one speaks about « economic union », almost everybody thinks of an improvement of the coordination of econo-

---

2 Ibid., p. 3.
3 H. Van Rompuy, in close collaboration with J.-M. Barroso, J.-C. Juncker and M. Draghi : « Towards a Genuine Economic and Monetary Union », 5 December 2012.

mic policies going in some cases to the adoption of common policies as well as the setting up of legal and budgetary instruments making this better coordination possible. This institutional dimension is of course essential but we should not lose sight of the other dimension, what I would call the structural dimension. An economic union is first of all a single market that should be truly integrated and completed. The two dimensions are equally important; if one is missing, we have no true economic union.

Now there is a paradox that is rarely recognised but that Mario Monti has well underlined : several euro-area members, including the biggest, are lagging behind in comparison with countries which do not participate in EMU. According to this experienced observer, « countries like the United Kingdom, Denmark, Sweden (…) are more compliant with the rules of the single market, the competition and the state aids (…) than most euro-area countries »[4]. We should put an end to this paradox. The euro-area countries, to begin with Germany and France, should be the first to encourage the effective achievement of a single market for electricity, rail transport or insurance. They should be the first to comply without restriction with the rules of the single market. They should be the first because a single market is a structural component of a monetary union.

This is especially true when the challenge is to build a « Capital Markets Union ». Granted, a single capital market could be useful for the whole European Union, but it is absolutely critical in a monetary union : conducting a single monetary policy in an area with broadly varying financial practices is difficult and sometimes dangerous. Therefore, « financial integration of the countries in EMU must receive top priority in a process that the rest of the European Union may then subsequently join »[5].

I come now to the institutional dimension. Even if the recent improvements I have mentioned go in the right direction, they are not sufficient. The experience of other monetary unions shows that, even if the degree of centralisation of fiscal instruments and the modalities of financial solidarity may be very different, the survival of a monetary union requires some form of common budget or, in the more prudent words of Herman Van

---

4 M. Monti : « Gouvernance économique : questions ouvertes », in L'Euro, les investisseurs et la gouvernance, Notre Europe, 2011, p. 66.
5 A. Brender, F. Pisani and D. Gros : « Building a Capital Markets Union…or designing a financial system for the euro area ? », CEPS Commentary, 2 June 2015.

Rompuy, some form of « *fiscal capacity* »[6] . Such mechanism could have three aims : first, to help Member States to implement necessary *structural reforms* which might generate costs before benefits (this was the original idea of Chancellor Merkel taken over by Herman Van Rompuy) ; second, to provide a temporary but significant transfer of resources in case of asymetric shocks, thereby reducing the financial and social cost of the adjustment for the countries concerned ; third, to be an instrument to counteract *severe recessions* in the area as a whole. The first aim was rejected by several governments who claim that they have already implemented important reforms and do not see why they should contribute to finance the reforms of others. The third aim appears for the moment too ambitious as it would require a bigger budget to be effective for the whole euro-area. Therefore I will focus on the second aim.

The creation of a shock absorbing mechanism is all the more necessary because *other corrective mechanisms play less in EMU* than in the US : despite some recent progress, *labour mobility* is much lower in Europe ; in stress time, *capital movements* can provoke a rapid fragmentation of financial markets, thus aggravating the difficulties of the countries hit by an asymetric shock ; *structural rigidities* can slow or even prevent the adjustment through prices. In this context, a fiscal capacity for the euro-area in view of helping to absorb asymetric shocks appears fully justified as far as it respects some principles. I insist on three of these principles:

1. This mechanism for helping to address country-specific shocks should be structured in such a way that it does not lead to permanent unidirectional transfers between countries. Over time, each country, as it moves along its economic cycle, would in turn be a net recipient or a net contributor of the scheme. This is what Guntram Wolff calls the principle of *distributional neutrality*: no net transfer in the long run[7]. If such a mechanism would have existed since the introduction of the eu-

---

6 H. Van Rompuy and al. : op. cit. It is interesting to note that a group of eleven German economists – the Glienicker Group – stated that « the monetary union cannot be permanently stable without a controlled transfer mechanism (…) to cushion the fiscal consequences of a dramatic economic downturn », Die Zeit, 17 October 2013. See also the joint document of the German and French ministers for Economy, S. Gabriel and E. Macron : « un budget commun à l'échelle de la zone euro (…) est la condition de l'efficacité de notre union monétaire », Le Soir, 4 June 2015.
7 G. Wolff : « A Budget for Europe's Monetary Union », Bruegel Policy Contribution, December 2012, p. 6.

ro, it would have benefited the countries in the North of the euro-area in the early years of the century and it would have benefited the countries in the South after 2009.

2. The existence of such a mechanism should not encourage countries to postpone the necessary reforms to address national structural weaknesses. To the contrary, it is important to ensure that any future asymmetric shock does not stem from non-cooperative structural policies. Therefore I suggest that the implementation of the *country-specific recommendations* issued by the Council in the framework of the « European semester » should be a prior condition to benefit from the mechanism.

3. The mechanism should not be redundant with the European Stability Mechanism (ESM) which has been established, as I said, to manage an acute crisis when a country loses access to capital markets. The function of the fiscal capacity should be to improve the *economic resilience* of countries in order to prevent such acute crises. Therefore, it should make ESM interventions much rarer.

Of course three important questions must be solved: What would trigger the intervention of the euro-area budget in favour of a specific country? What would be the amount of the intervention? And how would this budget be funded?

Should the intervention of the euro-area budget be automatic or based on discretion? Ideally, discretion would seem preferable to address specific shocks in a targeted way. However, discretion implies a strong decision-making center that would be able to take decisions quickly and that would be fully accountable to a democratic watchdog. Such an institutional setting does not yet exist; it would require important Treaty changes which do not seem feasible in the near future. Therefore, I think that we have to look for some kind of automatic stabilisers which would enter into motion according to clear ex ante rules. We could think of several indicators which could be used to trigger the intervention of the euro-area budget: a decline in *GDP* significantly sharper than the average of the euro-area; an increase of the *rate of unemployment* (or of the rate of unemployment for less than 12 months in order to capture the most cyclical component of unemployment[8]) significantly stronger than the evolution for the whole euro-

---

8 See Chart 4 : Cyclical nature of unemployment by benefit duration period, in Trésor-Economics, n° 132, June 2014, p. 5.

area; an enlargement of the *output gap* significantly bigger than the evolution for the whole euro-area; a significant deviation of the *interest rate on sovereign bonds* from the average interest rate. Each indicator has its advantages and its drawbacks; some, like the output gap, cannot be observed or estimated accurately in real time and are often revised substantially over time[9]. Several indicators could be used in combination. What is certain is that we must reason in terms of differences in evolution, not in absolute level.

What would be the amount of the intervention? The amount should be high enough to provide a real relief to the country in shock by easing its borrowing requirements and making its fiscal policy less procyclical. However, the amount should not be too high to ensure that the intervention does not create any incentive to artificially prolong the duration of the negative evolution at its origin. This means that the intervention of the euro-area budget should always be *temporary* and its amount should be *smaller* than the actual cost of the negative evolution for the national budget. For example, the euro-area budget could pay 70% of the additional expenditures in unemployment benefits for 12 months. So the country concerned would have no incentive to increase the number of unemployed who actually receive benefits or the income replacement rate level (i.e. the percentage of the past earnings replaced by the unemployment benefit) as 30% of the additional cost would still be at its charge. On the other hand, the intervention of the euro-area budget would help the country in shock to maintain unemployment benefits as this type of expenditure is an important automatic stabilizer that attenuates the economic impact of cyclical shocks. The multiplier effect of unemployment benefits is very large since it primarily targets low-income households facing cash shortfalls.

A third important question is *how the euro-area budget should be funded*. Revenues could come from national budgets or from a specific EMU tax. Again, in an ideal world, I would suggest that the second option would be preferable. Taking into account the purpose of the mechanism, I would think that a small percentage on corporate profits would be an appropriate own ressource for the euro-area budget. As a first approximation, by using AMECO data on corporate earnings, we find that the average corporate tax rate that would have generated 0,6% of GDP in income

---

9 See G. Wolff : « potential output is a concept that is appealing in theory but controversial in practice », ibid., p. 10.

during 2002-2010 is 4,2%. But this would require a prior harmonisation of the tax base and we know that, despite the excellent work already done by the Commission, we are still far from an agreement on such an harmonisation. In their joint document, Ministers S. Gabriel and E. Macron suggest that this own resource might also be the tax on financial transactions. A Commission proposal is currently under discussion but only between 11 Member States. To transform it into an own resource for the euro-area would require an enlargement to all EMU members which should unanimously agree on the modalities of this new tax; what is far from achieved with 11 would be much more difficult with 19 and would be a very lenghty process. Therefore, in the meantime, I see no other solution than to fund the budget with national contributions. According to some estimates[10], this budget should amount to 1% of the euro-area GDP, i.e. some 100 billions, in order to be able to play its shock-absorbing role but I think that it could be smaller provided that it would have a borrowing capacity constrained with a strict structural balanced budget rule (i.e. over the cycle)[11].

In summary, the creation of a fiscal capacity is of major importance for the good functioning of EMU. Fiscal support is needed to address severe shocks and alleviate the financial and social cost of adjustment. The very existence of such a mechanism would send a strong signal which would reduce the ex ante likelihood that a Member State will be affected by self-fulfilling prophecies. It would strengthen the euro-area substantially.

Agreeing on ex ante rules and contributions for an automatic support system would require only a relatively limited degree of further political integration. Article 352 of the Treaty allows the adoption of measures in areas where the Treaty currently does not explicitly provide all necessary powers to reach the Treaty objectives; it could therefore possibly be a suitable Treaty base.

Of course, at a later stage, a more ambitious fiscal union would be desirable. But we know that the European integration can only move forward step by step. The step I suggest today is not the end of the road but it would be a significant move in the right direction.

(published online mid-June 2015)

---

10 G. Wolff : Ibid., p. 11.
11 The Glienicker Group proposes « to finance the euro-budget through a membership fee, in the amount of about 0.5 per cent of the gross domestic product », Die Zeit, 17 October 2013.

L'européanisation des politiques énergétiques des pays membres de l'Union européenne: un processus lent mais inévitable

Laurent Baechler

Evidence des synergies et nécessité de la coopération

La politique énergétique européenne naissante est articulée autour de trois priorités clairement établies par le Traité de Lisbonne : la sécurité énergétique, entendue comme la sécurisation des approvisionnements à prix raisonnables ; la compétitivité des marchés énergétiques, qui doit contribuer à la baisse des prix de l'énergie et au dynamisme des économies européennes ; la protection du climat, qui passe par une maîtrise des émissions de carbone. Ces trois objectifs ont leur logique propre, mais ils s'articulent dans un jeu à somme potentiellement fortement positive : maîtriser la consommation énergétique permet de réduire les émissions de carbone (sachant que deux-tiers des émissions de gaz à effet de serre sont liés à l'utilisation d'énergie) et d'augmenter la sécurité ; réduire les coûts d'accès à l'énergie permet d'améliorer la compétitivité des économies européennes et de renforcer la sécurité énergétique ; développer les énergies renouvelables permet de lutter contre le réchauffement global, de réduire la dépendance aux énergies fossiles et d'améliorer la compétitivité des économies européennes.

L'existence de ces synergies évidentes rend étonnant le fait que les politiques énergétiques ne figurent à l'agenda européen que depuis une date très récente : le premier Conseil européen véritablement consacré aux questions énergétiques remonte à février 2011… Il est pourtant clair qu'il s'agit là d'un domaine où la nécessité de coopération pour apporter des réponses aux problèmes posés paraît s'imposer. Les exemples abondent pour le démontrer : dans le domaine des infrastructures, où l'interconnexion des réseaux impose de fait la coopé- ration ; en matière d'harmonisation des politiques nationales, qui ont des répercussions sur l'éventail de choix des partenaires (la transition énergétique allemande modifie les coûts d'approvisionnement énergétique des autres pays membres, par exemple) ; en matière de lutte contre le réchauffement climatique, où rien ne peut se faire si ce n'est à l'échelle européenne (en fait planétaire) ; en termes de financement des investissements en rapport avec la stratégie énergétique européenne (estimés par exemple à 60-70 milliards d'euros annuels pour atteindre l'objectif en matière de renouvelables d'ici 2020) ; dans le domaine de la recherche (sur les énergies renouvelables ou le stockage du carbone), où la mise en commun des moyens permettrait de dégager des synergies importantes.

Des exigences nouvelles s'imposant aux pays membres de l'UE

L'émergence récente de ces préoccupations communes s'explique par l'apparition de pressions externes qui, comme souvent dans le processus d'intégration européenne, ont conduit les Etats membres de l'UE à réviser leur stratégie nationale respective. Les élargissements à l'Est ont tout d'abord considérablement augmenté le taux de dépendance énergétique extérieure, et ce particulièrement vis-à-vis de la Russie, qui représente désormais environ 40% des importations européennes de gaz naturel et 35% des importations de pétrole. Cette dépendance extérieure s'est accompagnée d'une forte instabilité des approvisionnements, comme l'ont rappelé depuis 2006 les multiples crises entre la Russie et l'Ukraine et leurs répercussions en matière d'importation de gaz à l'est de l'UE. La forte augmentation du prix des énergies fossiles dans les années 2000 sous la poussée du décollage économique chinois a également joué un rôle important. La détente actuelle des prix apporte un répit relatif, dans la mesure où la dépendance européenne aux importations d'énergies fossiles ne devrait faire qu'augmenter dans les années à venir (il est prévu que l'UE importe 85% de son gaz naturel et 93% de son pétrole en 2030, sans réorientation profonde de sa stratégie énergétique). Enfin la « révolution » nord-américaine du gaz de schiste a changé la donne, en accentuant la perte de compétitivité énergétique européenne. Le processus en est à ses débuts, mais le passage prévisible de l'économie américaine du statut d'importateur à celui de puissance autonome (voir d'exportateur) sur le plan énergétique devrait peser sur les perspectives de croissance comparée des deux zones.

Pour toutes ces raisons, combinées aux synergies précédemment évoquées, les pays membres de l'UE sont de plus en plus amenés à considérer leur avenir énergétique en commun. La solidarité de fait s'impose aux égoïsmes nationaux, et devrait faire émerger une vision de l'Europe énergétique dans laquelle il est de moins en moins concevable que les pays membres résolvent leurs problèmes énergétiques exclusivement par des solutions nationales.

Des obstacles encore nombreux à la coopération

Le défi de la coopération énergétique est cependant de taille, étant donné la situation de départ qui se caractérise par des politiques énergétiques nationales très hétéroclites, tant sur le plan des instruments que des objectifs. L'énergie est un domaine stratégique, et le fait que les Etats membres de l'UE ont souhaité jusqu'ici conserver leurs prérogatives nationales pour mener à leur guise leur stratégie énergétique est à la fois une cause et une conséquence de ce que l'on peut constater dans ce domaine : un patchwork de situations et de préférences nationales, articulation de contraintes géologiques et géopolitiques. On trouve ainsi dans l'Union des pays importateurs ou exportateurs d'énergie, des bouquets énergétiques très différents d'un pays à l'autre, des stratégies de sortie du nucléaire ou de maintien du parc, des positions très différentes sur l'exploitation du potentiel en gaz de schiste, des situations très disparates en matière de connexion aux réseaux d'infrastructures énergétiques européennes, ainsi qu'en matière de dépendance énergétique vis-à-vis des différents fournisseurs extérieurs d'énergie, des pays dotés de « champions nationaux » en matière énergétique tandis que d'autres en sont dépourvus.

Ces disparités inévitables expliquent en grande partie qu'une volonté de politique européenne de l'énergie n'ait vu le jour que très récemment, et que les progrès en termes de coopération se manifestent dans certains domaines davantage que dans d'autres. Si l'on retient les trois priorités précédemment évoquées, on peut considérer que la coopération est balbutiante en matière de sécurité, plus solide dans le domaine de la compétitivité, et avancée pour ce qui concerne la protection du climat. En matière de sécurité énergétique, et notamment d'indépendance vis-à-vis des approvisionnements extérieurs, l'obstacle à la coopération vient principalement du fait que les Etats les plus influents souhaitent continuer de mener leur politique étrangère énergétique en toute indépendance, via principalement leurs « champions nationaux ». La coopération dans ce domaine se limite à quelques projets d'infrastructures considérés comme d'intérêt commun (corridor Sud-Est pour développer l'accès au gaz de la mer caspienne, plan solaire destiné à ouvrir un partenariat avec le sud et l'est de la Méditerranée sur les renouvelables). En matière de compétitivité, la création d'un marché européen de l'énergie fait partie de la stratégie plus large d'achèvement du marché intérieur, pour laquelle la nécessité de coopérer fait peu de doute. Les obstacles à la coopération peuvent ici être différents : ils relèvent des coûts de mise en œuvre des infrastructures de connexion des réseaux nationaux, des résistances nationales à la dérégle- mentation des marchés de l'énergie, ou tout simplement des échecs cons- tatés de la stratégie (comme par exemple la hausse des prix de l'énergie succédant à la libéralisation des marchés énergétiques). C'est donc princi- palement dans le domaine de l'articulation entre politique énergétique et politique climatique que la coopération européenne se manifeste de la ma- nière la plus évidente, au point que l'UE dispose déjà d'instruments fédéraux pour atteindre ses objectifs, comme le marché européen des per- mis d'émission de carbone. La coopération est ici indispensable pour fixer les objectifs de réduction des émissions de gaz à effet de serre, mais elle tend à se diffuser dans l'articulation des instruments nécessaires pour at- eindre ces objectifs, comme par exemple en matière de développement des énergies renouvelables ou d'investissements dans l'amélioration de l'effi- cacité énergétique.

On peut donc s'attendre à ce qu'à court terme, la consolidation de la po- litique européenne de l'énergie passe principalement par le biais climati- que, avant que les dimensions de sécurité énergétique et de compétitivité ne viennent compléter le dispositif.

(published online mid-November 2014)

La politique climatique de l'Union européenne au pied du mur

Laurent Baechler

Dans la perspective de la Conférence des Parties de la Convention-Cadre des Nations Unies sur les Changements Climatiques prévue à Paris en décembre 2015 pour parvenir à un traité international devant succéder au Protocole de Kyoto, l'Union européenne a récemment réitéré ses ambitions en matière de lutte contre le changement climatique. En remplacement de la stratégie 3 x 20 précédente, les objectifs communs désormais affichés sont les suivants : réduction d'au moins 40% des émissions de gaz à effet de serre (GES) à l'horizon 2030 par rapport à 1990 ; augmentation de la part des énergies renouvelables à 27% du paquet énergétique européen ; amélioration de 27% de l'efficacité énergétique des économies européennes. Tout ceci toujours dans la perspective plus lointaine de pouvoir réduire les émissions européennes de GES de 80 à 95% d'ici 2050, ce qui correspond à l'objectif proposé par le Groupe d'experts intergouvernemental sur l'évolution du climat (GIEC) de contenir le réchauffement global à long terme à $2°$ C (à condition bien sûr que les autres pays participent à l'effort à hauteur souhaitée), limite considérée comme supportable pour la biosphère et les systèmes humains.

Ces objectifs ambitieux s'inscrivent dans la ligne de conduite adoptée depuis une quinzaine d'année par l'UE en matière de politique climatique, qui l'a amenée à devenir le chef de file des négociations climatiques internationales et le modèle à suivre en matière de politique climatique. Ce rôle de modèle se justifie en partie par les performances obtenues jusqu'ici en matière de maîtrise des émissions de GES. Le Protocole de Kyoto, adopté en 1997, attribuait en effet à l'UE (15) l'objectif de réduire ses émissions de GES de 8% entre 1990 et la période 2008-2012[1]. Cet objectif fut atteint dès 2005, et la performance finalement réalisée fut une réduction de près

---

[1] 8% était la cible moyenne, chaque pays membre se voyant attribuer un objectif propre en fonction de ses performances passées et de ses capacités à contribuer à l'effort collectif. Ainsi la France avait par exemple pour objectif de stabiliser ses émissions sur la période.

de 19%[2], bien au-delà de ce que les « partenaires » de l'UE furent capables d'obtenir. Les autres pays concernés par les objectifs quantifiés de Kyoto[3] se sont effectivement révélés en grande partie incapables d'atteindre leur cible, le mauvais élève en la matière étant le Canada, qui devait réduire ses émissions de 6% mais les a laissées augmenter de 30%. Certains comme le Japon y sont parvenus, mais à la faveur d'un ralentissement économique prolongé accentué par la crise de 2008.

Le rôle de moteur des négociations internationales a permis à l'UE d'enregistrer par le passé des succès incontestables. Le plus remarquable étant la formation d'une coalition d'Etats permettant l'entrée en vigueur du Protocole de Kyoto en 2005 en l'absence de participation des Etats-Unis[4], à la faveur de la ratification par des acteurs auparavant réticents, et finalement convaincus par l'Europe de participer à l'effort collectif, à savoir le Canada, le Japon et finalement la Russie. Mais les circonstances actuelles sont bien différentes de ce qu'elles étaient dans la première moitié des années 2000. Parvenir à un accord post-Kyoto devant entrer en vigueur à partir de 2020 nécessite aujourd'hui la pleine participation des deux plus gros émetteurs de GES, la Chine (premier émetteur désormais avec 25% des émissions globales) et les Etats-Unis (15%). Si l'on ajoute à cela le fait que la motivation des autres pays pour participer à l'effort collectif s'est émoussée pour des raisons diverses (le Japon post-Fukushima n'entend plus être aussi ambitieux que ce qu'il avait annoncé à la conférence de Copenhague en 2009, la Russie en conflit avec l'Occident n'est plus dans les mêmes dispositions, le Canada s'est retiré du processus de Kyoto en 2011 et annonce depuis des objectifs faiblement ambitieux), et que le poids de l'UE dans les émissions mondiales de GES a fortement diminué avec la croissance accélérée des pays émergents (il est passé de plus de 18% des émissions totales en 1990 à près de 10% aujourd'hui), force est de constater que la capacité de l'UE à mobiliser les efforts inter-

---

2 A la suite des élargissements de 2004 et 2007, les objectifs précédemment attribués aux nouveaux Etats membres furent repris par l'UE. Seuls Chypre et Malte n'avaient pas d'obligation en matière de réduction des émissions de GES.

3 Les pays dits de l'annexe 1 du Protocole, essentiellement les pays riches ou en transition post-soviétique. Les Etats-Unis, n'ayant pas ratifié le Protocole de Kyoto et s'étant retirés des négociations internationales en mars 2001, n'étaient pas concernés.

4 L'entrée en vigueur du Protocole de Kyoto nécessitait sa ratification par des Etats représentant au moins 55% des émissions mondiales de GES. Ce seuil fut atteint suite à la ratification Russe en février 2005.

nationaux pour réduire les émissions de GES s'est fortement amoindrie au cours de la dernière décennie. L'ultime atout qui lui reste en la matière est de tenir ses engagements de réduction d'émissions de GES, qui demeurent de loin les plus ambitieux à long terme, et de continuer de jouer ainsi le rôle de modèle en matière de politique climatique.

La partie n'est pas gagnée, loin s'en faut. Les performances passées reposaient sur des objectifs relativement modestes, et ceux-ci ont été atteints en partie grâce à des évolutions fortuites sans rapport avec les instruments de politique climatique mis en œuvre. Le problème auquel fait face actuellement l'UE en la matière peut donc se résumer de la manière suivante : comment atteindre les objectifs extrêmement ambitieux fixés pour 2050, alors que les opportunités des réductions des émissions de GES les plus faciles ont déjà été exploitées par le passé, et que les performances réalisées jusqu'ici reposent en partie sur des effets d'aubaine ?

L'objectif affiché pour 2050 consiste en une réduction des émissions de GES à l'échelle européenne de 80 à 95%, soit une division par 5 à 20 des émissions globales par rapport au niveau de 1990[5]! Rappelons que pour la première période d'application du Protocole de Kyoto, l'objectif européen n'était « que » de réduire les émissions de 8% sur une période de près de 25 ans. Si l'on ajoute à cela le fait qu'en l'absence de bond technologique majeur, il sera de plus en plus difficile de réduire les émissions de GES à mesure que le niveau global diminuera[6], on mesure l'ampleur du défi que l'UE s'est lancée à elle-même pour les décennies à venir. Mais ce n'est pas tout. Les performances enregistrées jusqu'ici sont en grande partie le résultat d'événements fortuits qui se sont produits dans les deux principaux pays émetteurs de GES de l'UE, l'Allemagne et le Royaume-Uni, et qui se sont répercutés sur les émissions européennes. En Allemagne, la réunification a eu pour effet de moderniser les cinq nouveaux Länder et d'y réduire l'intensité carbone des installations de production de chaleur et d'électricité, contribuant ainsi aux performances moyennes du pays. Au Royaume-Uni, c'est la substitution du gaz naturel au pétrole et au charbon pour la production d'électricité qui a contribué à la réduction de émissions

---

5 Depuis les négociations sur le Protocole de Kyoto dans les années 1990, 1990 est l'année de base retenue pour tous les calculs d'objectifs en la matière.

6 A technologie inchangée, le « rendement » de réduction des émissions de GES ne peut être que décroissant, les opportunités de réduction les plus aisées étant exploitées en premier, l'effort nécessaire pour poursuivre les réductions augmentant progressivement.

de carbone[7]. Cet effet d'aubaine est pour beaucoup dans l'atteinte des objectifs européens de Kyoto, même s'il reste très difficile de le mesurer avec précision. Or, depuis, l'UE a renforcé ses ambitions, avec comme objectif intermédiaire récemment adopté la réduction des émissions de GES d'au moins 40% pour 2030[8].

Les instruments avec lesquels l'UE compte atteindre ces objectifs sont nombreux, mais l'essentiel repose encore sur le marché des crédits carbone lancé en 2005. Celui-ci est en effet censé contribuer aux deux tiers à la réalisation de l'objectif intermédiaire 2030. Le reste repose sur une série de mesures appelées « politiques et mesures communes coordonnées » (treize mesures en tout), et qui vont de la réduction des émissions des véhicules individuels à l'amélioration des performances énergétiques des bâtiments, en passant par la taxation de l'énergie. Qu'il s'agisse de l'objectif intermédiaire 2030 ou de l'objectif final 2050, la capacité de ces mesures à contribuer à les atteindre reste à prouver, le manque de recul en la matière interdisant toute conclusion. Les choses sont plus claires en ce qui concerne la contribution du marché des crédits carbone, dans la mesure où le dispositif repose sur ce que l'on appelle un système « cap-and-trade », autrement dit la fixation d'un quota global d'émissions de carbone associé à un marché d'échange de crédits carbone entre les acteurs concernés, ceux-ci représentant actuellement environ 11000 installations industrielles, soit près de 50% des émissions de GES dans l'UE. Le projet européen est de réduire ce quota global de 1,74% par an entre 2005 et 2020 (et de poursuivre par la suite), pour atteindre une réduction totale d'émissions de 21% dans les secteurs concernés par ce marché carbone d'ici 2020. Contrairement à ce qui est envisageable avec les « politiques et mesures communes coordonnées »[9], les autorités européennes s'appuient là sur un levier direct, puisqu'elles fixent elles-mêmes un objectif contraignant de réduction des émissions de GES à l'échelle de l'UE. Encore faut-il que le dispositif soit efficace, ce qui n'est pas le cas jusqu'à présent. Pour être

---

7 La raison en est l'effet prix suite à la libéralisation des marchés britanniques de l'énergie. L'intensité carbone du gaz naturel est inférieure à celle du pétrole, et très inférieure à celle du charbon.

8 Objectif qui pour de nombreux observateurs est en-deçà de ce qu'il faudrait proposer pour rester en phase avec l'objectif 2050.

9 Ces mesures permettent effectivement d'orienter certains comportements émetteurs de GES par le biais d'incitations ou de réglementations contraignantes, sans qu'il soit possible de mesurer a priori leur impact sur les émissions in fine.

pleinement opérationnel, un marché de permis négociables de ce genre doit reposer sur une contrainte forte imposée aux pollueurs (autrement dit il doit leur fournir moins de permis que ce dont ils ont besoin habituellement), pour les obliger à acheter ces permis même si leur prix augmente fortement. Or jusqu'ici, le prix du carbone sur le marché européen a subi des fluctuations accompagnées de chutes fréquentes. Une explication est la faible contrainte imposée aux émetteurs de carbone, les quotas distribués par les autorités nationales étant trop généreux. Une autre est l'impact de la crise sur l'activité économique en Europe et la réduction du besoin de permis qu'elle entraîne pour les acteurs concernés. Ce marché est la pierre angulaire de la stratégie climatique européenne, et son bon fonctionnement est indispensable pour atteindre les objectifs fixés. Les chances en la matière dépendent en partie de la capacité des autorités européennes à imposer un dispositif efficace, ainsi que de la bonne volonté des Etats membres à se plier à la discipline collective.

Le bilan de la politique climatique européenne est donc contrasté. Les performances réalisées sont jusqu'ici satisfaisantes, mais s'expliquent en partie par des éléments exogènes, alors qu'elles reposaient sur des objectifs modestes. L'avenir s'annonce plus difficile, avec des cibles beaucoup plus ambitieuses et des instruments plus compliqués à mobiliser.

(published online end of April 2015)

Europe's member states

Sortir de la zone euro et revenir au franc ou l'assurance d'un échec annoncé!

Jean-Claude Vérez

Outre le fait que le retour aux monnaies nationales comme le franc français est préconisé voire réclamé par les anti-européens, il y a bien longtemps que les opposants à l'euro ont mobilisé plusieurs arguments économiques pour dire tout le mal qu'ils pensaient de la monnaie unique. Mais en cette fin d'année 2014, l'essentiel n'est pas là ; ce qui importe depuis la crise de 2007-2008 tient aux secousses qui ont frappé l'Union européenne, aux difficultés de retrouver la croissance et le plein emploi et aux tentations d'un trio infernal : replis nationaux, néoprotectionnisme et rétablissement des monnaies nationales.

En France, les extrêmes sur l'échiquier politique ne sont pas opposés au franc espérant retrouver ainsi une autonomie de leur politique monétaire. Il existe pourtant de nombreux obstacles pour que l'abandon de l'euro ne se transforme en crise économique (voire politique) majeure. Déjà, au moment de la supposée sortie de la Grèce de l'euro, les investisseurs avaient manifesté leur inquiétude. Rappelons comme le précisent les statuts de l'Union européenne (UE) que l'euro n'est pas seulement une monnaie unique, une monnaie de transaction et une monnaie de réserve, c'est aussi le symbole d'une union politique.

Au-delà des problèmes techniques source de coûts supplémentaires (remplacer les billets libellés en euro par des billets libellés en franc), la première interrogation porte sur le nouveau taux de change avec les monnaies à statut international que sont le dollar, l'euro qui continuerait à exister, le yen ou encore la livre sterling et le franc suisse. Sauf erreur, l'intérêt d'une telle configuration tient à un franc déprécié par rapport à la valeur actuelle de l'euro. Cette dépréciation constitue de façon évidente une source d'une meilleure compétitivité prix. À l'exportation, les produits made in France se vendraient mieux. Il reste toutefois à satisfaire trois conditions : 1/ Que la demande mondiale soit élastique par rapport au prix. 2/ Que l'appareil productif soit en capacité de produire en quantités supérieures pour faire face à la nouvelle demande mondiale. 3/ Que les biens et/ou services nationaux destinés à l'export ne soient pas contraints dans leur processus de fabrication d'importer des matières premières ou autres in-trants étrangers dont le coût libellé en dollars ou en euros aurait mécani-quement augmenté du fait de la dépréciation du franc par rapport aux monnaies citées.

Prenons un exemple fictif : **1€ s'échange contre 1,30$**, soit 1$ contre 0,77€. Si le FF lors de sa mise en circulation est estimé à 0,80€ compte tenu de l'effet escompté, le nouveau taux de change devient : 1FF = 0,80€ soit 1€ = 1,25FF. Comme 1 € s'échange contre 1,30$, on obtient 1,25 FF = 1,30$. On peut donc écrire : 1FF = 1,04$. Quand un américain à Paris achetait une baguette à **1€**, il lui fallait débourser **1,30$**. Avec le retour du franc, quand il achète la même baguette, il lui « suffit » de débourser 1,04$ soit une économie de 20 %. La baguette française est donc bien plus compétitive.

Simultanément, un français qui achetait un hamburger à New York au prix d'1$ devait sortir de son porte-monnaie 0,77€. Avec le nouveau taux de change (1FF = 1,04$), il devra sortir 0,96FF. Toute importation libellée en dollar engendre de facto un surcoût de 25 % On comprend donc que le prix de nos importations incompressibles comme le pétrole ou le gaz vont se répercuter sur le pouvoir d'achat des ménages et sur les coûts de pro-duction des entreprises nationales.

On a donc la certitude que le retour au franc sur la base d'1FF inférieur à 1€ aurait pour conséquence immédiate un renchérissement des biens im-portés. On peut se demander si le FF serait nécessairement inférieur à 1€ ? Il suffit de rappeler que les opposants à l'euro ont entre autres arguments le fait que la monnaie européenne est trop forte par rapport au dollar et plus encore par rapport au yuan chinois. Substituer le FF à l'euro n'aurait donc de sens que s'il était plus « faible » face au dollar que l'euro. Ce nou-veau contexte aboutirait en outre à des pressions inflationnistes qui pour-raient « faire « boule de neige ». La hausse des produits importés se réper-cuterait sur les prix domestiques pour les ménages (l'essence coûterait plus chère) et sur les coûts de production, lesquels à leur tour se répercute-raient sur les prix de détail de sorte que le pouvoir d'achat finirait par bais-ser sérieusement.

Le deuxième défi posé par le retour au franc concerne les monnaies de réserve des banques centrales. Depuis la création de l'euro, deux monnaies constituent l'essentiel des réserves des banques centrales.

Le dollar constitue 61 % des réserves depuis 2010 et l'euro 26 %. La livre sterling, le yen, le franc suisse et les autres monnaies ne « pèsent » qu'un peu plus de 10 %. On comprend assez vite ce que pèserait le franc

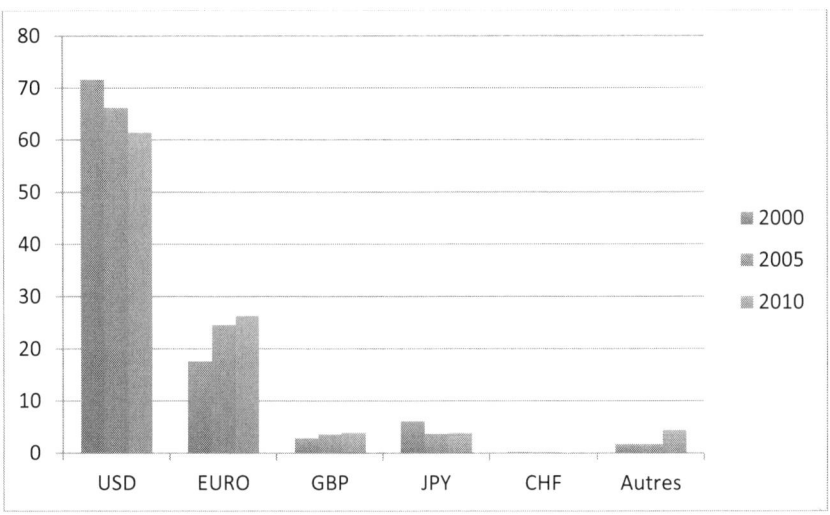

Figure 1 : Part respective des monnaies dans les réserves de change

français dans les réserves mondiales. Si le dollar reste **La** monnaie internationale par excellence, on constate le poids croissant de l'euro, ce qui signifie que les acteurs internationaux lui accordent une certaine confiance dont la Chine. Cette confiance est de nature à attirer des capitaux et à emprunter à des taux d'intérêt plus bas.

Le troisième défi est justement lié au poids de notre dette qui approche les 100 % du PIB. Le passage au franc impacterait de facto le volume de la dette extérieure qui resterait libellé en euros tandis que le franc serait moins fort que la monnaie européenne. Par ailleurs, la France malgré ses problèmes structurels, continue en 2014 à obtenir la confiance des prêteurs qui ne contestent pas sa signature. En irait-il de même si elle sortait de l'euro? Rien n'est moins sûr de sorte qu'emprunter se ferait à un taux d'intérêt plus élevé et, donc, à un coût plus élevé. En introduisant une nouvelle monnaie, l'économie française verrait sa crédibilité affectée synonyme d'une prime de risque plus forte sur sa dette extérieure. À l'opposé, la France verrait sa dette intérieure plus facile à payer du fait de sa monnaie sous-évaluée. L'État pourrait ainsi se libérer du poids de la dette avec un peu moins de contrainte. Reste à savoir lequel des deux effets cités aurait le plus d'impact sur les indicateurs macro-économiques.

Avec une monnaie affaiblie par rapport à l'euro, les épargnants seraient les grands perdants du retour au franc. Ce quatrième défi n'est pas le moins difficile. Si certains y voient un moyen de ruiner les rentiers dans un contexte de lutte des classes, d'autres y décèlent une fuite des capitaux et des difficultés majeures à mobiliser l'épargne indispensable au financement des investissements des entreprises. En outre, on peut supposer que les hauts salaires synonymes de forte propension à épargner auraient plutôt des envies d'aller voir ailleurs. Cela pourrait se traduire par une fuite partielle des cerveaux, des hauts diplômés.

Sur le plan politique vis-à-vis de nos partenaires, le retour au franc ne pourrait qu'engendrer des désillusions. On ne peut pas faire comme si nous étions seuls à agir ou à décider. Outre les problèmes juridiques, les contraintes relatives aux traités auxquels nous sommes associés ou encore les modalités de fonctionnement de l'Union européenne, c'est évidemment la perte de confiance en la France qui serait le plus préjudiciable du point de vue diplomatique et du point de vue de nos relations internationales, à commencer par nos relations européennes. Le poids économique de la France dans le PIB européen reste substantiel ainsi que sa contribution au budget. Certes, une sortie de l'euro ne signifie pas de facto un retrait complet de tous les engagements français envers l'Union européenne mais qui peut nier le coup fatal que cette sortie impliquerait ? Comment ne pas y voir un renoncement à la construction européenne ?

Pour finir, il est acquis que la mondialisation est en marche et qu'elle ne va pas s'arrêter du jour au lendemain. Il est acquis encore qu'un basculement du monde s'opère sous nos yeux au profit, pour le moment, d'une partie de l'Asie. Qu'on la soutienne ou qu'on la déplore, cette mondialisation impose des nouvelles règles du jeu. L'affronter, y prendre part, l'impulser exige des moyens financiers, technologiques et humains via les qualifications et les compétences des ressources humaines. Peut-on imaginer l'Union européenne amputée de l'un de ses pays fondateurs y faire face ? Pourquoi pas ? Peut-on imaginer la France, repliée sur elle-même, plus protectionniste qu'ouverte aux échanges extérieurs y faire face à son tour avec une monnaie affaiblie ? Aurait-elle les moyens de rivaliser avec la compétitivité accrue des pays émergents dans un contexte de technologies sans cesse renouvelées ? On comprend que ces interrogations interpellent les supporters de la sortie de l'euro. Qu'à chacune de celles-ci, ils puissent nous apporter la preuve que le retour au franc est la meilleure solution pour résoudre nos difficultés. Et si tel est le cas, on veut bien réviser notre point de vue.

(published online end of September 2014)

Is France still a pivotal power in the EU? Reflections on the country's declining agenda-setting role

Matthias Waechter

"You don't do what is necessary." In Europe, you have the best geographical position. You don't have a political handicap as we have, since you were on the side of the winners of World War II. You keep an international influence, which is higher than your real power [...]. You have the best set of cards in your hands in order to be the first power in Europe. You should be the first power in Europe, but you don't do what is necessary."[1] These words don't date from these days, but were pronounced in 1974. It was Helmut Schmidt, Chancellor of the Federal Republic of Germany, who admonished the newly elected French President Valéry Giscard d'Estaing to play a more assertive role in Europe and to assume the leadership within the European institutions.

The issues raised by Schmidt have not lost their pertinence, though the map of Europe has profoundly changed since then. The European Union has enlarged to 28 member states; Germany has been reunified and grown demographically and economically. However, the assets for a French leadership in the EU remain virtually unchanged. It still is the only country, which due to its geographical position, can build a bridge between the Southern, Northern and Western states of the EU. It is, together with the UK, the only member state with a permanent seat on the UN Security Council and disposing of nuclear weapons. Its weight in international organisations like the World Bank and the International Monetary Found is considerable. It can look back on a century-old tradition of skilful diplomacy and a forward-thinking foreign policy.

However, the vast majority of observers would agree that France is currently falling behind as to its role as a European leader. From all corners of the EU, its government receives exhortations to finally engage into structural reforms, which should make the country fit for future chal-

---

1 Helmut Schmidt quoted in: Valéry Giscard d'Estaing, Le pouvoir et la vie, Vol. I, Paris 1988, p. 136.

lenges. The French nominee for Commissioner for Economic Affairs, Pierre Moscovici, struggled to gain his approval from the European Parliament, because several deputies were not convinced of his capacities to oversee budgetary discipline in Europe. Since the May 2014 elections, 23 out of the 74 French deputies of the European Parliament belong to the far-right Front National, not attached to any of the political groups and thus without an impact on the workings of the parliament.

When asked for the reasons of the decline of French leadership within the European Union, observers are inclined to give a seemingly evident response: It is because of the recent crisis and its repercussions on the French economy. With zero per cent growth, an unemployment rate of 9,7 per cent, and a budget deficit exceeding the commonly agreed threshold of 3 per cent, the country is now often labelled as the "sick man of Europe" and thus considered unsuitable for leadership within the EU. However, its economic problems are not a sufficient reason for the ineptness of France's current European policies. There is no causal link between economic success and European leadership, nor between economic slump and its absence. Certainly, the leverage of France would be higher if its economic performance was better, but this factor alone does not explain why the country is no longer identified as an agenda-setter in the EU.

The deeper causes of France's declining leadership are to be seen in an increasing désamour of the public for the idea of a supranational Europe. As numerous authors have convincingly demonstrated, European integration is no longer exclusively an elite-driven process accompanied by an indifferent public opinion. The times of the "permissive consensus" are over and have made place for a "restraining dissensus", as L. Hooghe and G. Marks have convincingly argued[2]. This finding is particularly true for France, where European politics are no longer part of the *domaine réservé* of the President of the Republic, but are negotiated in the public arena. Long before the outbreak of the financial and economic crisis, several indicators proved an increased alienation of the public from the integration process. From the presidential elections of 2002 is mostly remembered the staggering qualification of Jean-Marie Le Pen for the second round. It is, however, often forgotten that in the first round of the elections, 42 % of the voters expressed their preference for candidates fiercely or moderately

---

2 Liesbet Hooghe/Gary Marks, A Postfunctionalist Theory of European Integration: From Permissive Consensus to Constraining Dissensus, in: British Journal of Political Science 39 (2009), p. 1-23.

opposed to European integration[3]. The referendum on the Constitutional Treaty three years after only reinforced an already existing trend: A strong minority within the Socialist Party around Laurent Fabius had in the meantime discovered the electoral potential of Euroscepticism and declared its opposition to the treaty. The 54,6 % of votes against the constitutional treaty demonstrated the strength of anti-EU arguments from the left as well as from the right.

Since then, France has not overcome the shock of the constitutional referendum. Instead of encouraging the citizens to espouse again the idea of a supranational Europe, politicians have professed to "understand" the voters' alienation from the EU and have rhetorically flattered their Eurosceptic opinions. In this regard, the presidency of Nicolas Sarkozy constitutes a telling example: On the one hand, the president contributed significantly to the conclusion of the Lisbon treaty, on the other hand, he established at the same time a new Ministry devoted to "national identity" and avoided any principled commitment to supra-nationalism as a solution to France's current challenges. His rhetoric hailed an "economic patriotism" and let voters believe that the EU as a space of open borders was - at least partly - responsible for the country being allegedly "flooded" by immigrants.

Sarkozy's successor has certainly adopted a softer rhetoric on issues like immigration and national identity, but has not adopted a significantly new approach on communicating European integration to the citizens. In May 2013, François Hollande bluntly refused any interference of the European Commission into the country's internal affairs when stating that it had "not to dictate France what it has to do."[4] The night of the 2014 EP elections showed France's political leaders in a particularly disconcerted state, when their vast majority claimed they had "heard" the message which the voters had tried to convey to them by massively voting for Front National; however, virtually nobody engaged in rebutting and disproving the anti-EU propaganda of the far-right party.

In conclusion, the French political elite, as to its stance towards the EU, appears to be a prisoner of the Front National. In order not to loose voters

---

3 Aggregated votes for: Jean-Marie Le Pen, Bruno Megret, Robert Hue, Arlette Laguiller, Olivier Besancenot, Jean Saint-Josse, André Gluckstein and Jean-Pierre Chevènement.

4 Cf.: "Hollande: 'la Commission n'a pas à nous dicter ce que nous devons faire'", Le Point, 29/05/2014. http://www.lepoint.fr/economie/hollande-la-commission-n-a-pas -a-nous-dicter-ce-que-nous-avons-a-faire-29 -05-2013-1674318_28.php

to the extremist party, they don't dare to publicly commit to European integration and propose ambitious objectives for its agenda. Thus, French leadership is currently a victim of the domestic political arena of the country. Its restoration will certainly be facilitated by a better economic performance of the country. But only a patient, principled and unstinting pedagogical effort among its population will make it possible that France recovers its lost role as an agenda-setter for the EU.

(published online mid-October 2014)

Are all the French still "Charlie"?
Reflections after the terrorist attacks in Paris

Matthias Waechter

Anyone interested in the politics and society of France can only be amazed about the country's development in the last five weeks. Following the terrorist killings of 17 people in Paris on January 6th and 7th, an indolent, but deeply divided population suddenly wakes up and rallies for one of the biggest mass demonstrations in European history, adhering in large numbers to the slogan of national unity. A president with a record of unpopularity rises to statesman-like format when exhorting his fellow citizens to go back to their republican roots and collectively refrain from scapegoating. An unprecedented debate about the pertinence of France's secular values for today's society comes up, but rapidly dies out when the media begin to focus on other news. The time has thus come to suggest some analytical perspectives on those events, which have shaken France for several days. Among the many aspects relevant for social scientists, this paper looks at three issues around the Paris killings: The "national unity" of January 11th, the search for reasons of the terrorist attacks, and the possible future electoral consequences of the events.

The Moment of National Unity

In the months preceding the Charlie Hebdo attack, French society did not impress international observers by any widespread political agitation or civic activism. The disastrous results of the European Parliament elections of May 2014, which gave the right-wing extremist Front National for the first time ever the highest number of seats in a nation-wide election, did not trigger any remarkable reaction by public opinion. It seemed as if the rise of the populist, nationalist and xenophobic party was no longer scandalizing a majority of the French. A dull, uninvolved and silently permissive attitude prevailed among the population, very different from the situation in 2002, when Jean-Marie Le Pen's electoral success in the presidential election elicited massive civil protest.

Thus, the huge mobilisation after the attacks came undoubtedly as a surprise and asks for explanation, especially as previous terrorist acts, like Mohammed Merah's random killings in front of a Jewish school in Toulouse in 2012, did not provoke any comparable reactions on the part of the population. It is almost a truism to say that France is known for such sudden upsurges of political concern, rising from widespread public indifference. May 68 provides a good example for such a phenomenon: "Quand la France s'ennuie..." ran the headline of the newspaper *Le Monde* of March 15th 1968. "What currently characterizes our public life is boredom", stated editorialist Pierre Viansson-Ponté.[1] Six weeks later, the massive student and worker protests started, culminating in a general strike paralyzing the whole country. Typically for social movements in France, the mass mobilisation faded away as quickly as it had risen.[2]

But what happened exactly in the immediate aftermath of the killings, in order to help explaining us the extraordinary mass public mobilisation? It was President Hollande who played the key role, when he conveyed, in his speech broadcasted on the evening of the killings, his interpretation of the event. The massacred journalists were, according to the president, martyrs of their vision of France as the universal homestead of liberty. He sanctified the victims to "our heroes", worthy of a day of national mourning.[3] And he provided his reading of the terrorists' objectives: According to Hollande, their aim was to attack the Republic as a community of shared values, among them the freedom of expression, pluralism, and democracy. Thus, the president's speech can be described as an act of myth-making, in the sense that he tried to give an overarching meaning to the event, appealing to time-transcending ideas and powerful memories. The acts of the Kouachi brothers, probably primarily religiously motivated and targeted against journalists whom they perceived as blasphemous individuals, were reinterpreted as attacks on the French Republic and its citizens. The Charlie Hebdo journalists, who in their majority were irreverent

---

1 Pierre Viansson-Ponté, Quand la France s'ennuie...., Le Monde, 30.4.1968.
2 The slogans *Je suis Charlie - Nous sommes Charlie* recall the famous May 68 slogan *Nous sommes tous des juifs allemands*, which the protesting students chanted after Prime Minister Georges Pompidou had denounced their leader Daniel Cohn-Bendit as a "German Jew". The same formula of empathy and solidarity was taken up by *Le Monde*, which produced after the September 11th 2001 terrorist attacks the headline: *Nous sommes tous Américains*.
3 Full text of Hollande's speech from 7 January 2015 on: http://www.elysee.fr/declara tions/article/allocution-a-la-suite-de-l-attentat-au-siege-de-charlie-hebdo/.

towards any kind of ideologies and solemn discourses, were canonized by Hollande as republican heroes, driven by the certain "idea they had of France" - an expression taken directly from the vocabulary of Charles de Gaulle, founding father of the Fifth Republic. The president concluded his speech with a vigorous appeal to demonstrate "unity" faced with such adversity and to "rally" around the republican values. "Rassemblons-nous", exhorted Hollande his fellow citizens and thus evoked again powerful memories of Charles de Gaulle, whose buzzword was the "rassemblement" of all the French beyond all cleavages.[4]

The next step towards the mass political mobilisation was the reaction of those political forces opposing the president. With the exception of Front National and its leader Marine Le Pen, they all refrained from any politicking, wholeheartedly endorsed his interpretation of the events and his call to national unity. Some explicitly encouraged the public to close ranks around the president and help him in his defence of the French republic. Such a short-run increase of support is known in the American presidential system as the "Rally 'round the flag effect", regularly taking place when the country is perceived as being immediately threatened by an outside aggression.[5] The sudden domestic truce among deeply opposed political currents evoked again powerful memories among the French: The "sacred union" of August 1914, when all political forces suddenly stopped their constant bickering and unanimously endorsed the defence of the country against the German aggression. *Union sacrée* was the headline that several TV stations were running on 8th January 2015: One hundred years after the beginning of World War I, the nation seemed to have retrieved its capacity to unify when faced with unprecedented adversity.

The dramatic events of 9th January were the final trigger for the massive public mobilisation. When Amedy Coulibaly, after having shot a policewoman the day before, hijacked a cosher supermarket and killed in it four people, he confirmed the interpretation which Hollande had given to the Charlie Hebdo attack: Those events had a larger meaning than the Mohammed cartoon conflict, but concerned the rules, the values, even the possibility of living together in a republic. The President's speech on the night of 9th January set the tone for the upcoming mobilisation: He qualified the shootings now as attacks against France and the whole nation,

---

4 On the Gaullist tradition in France: Matthias Waechter, Der Mythos des Gaullismus. Heldenkult, Geschichtspolitik und Ideologie, Göttingen 2006.

5 Cf.: John E. Mueller, War, Presidents, and Public Opinion, New York 1973.

inviting to a mass rally in order to give a visual expression to the national unity to which he had constantly summoned.[6]

Thus, the reaction of the political leadership towards the terrorist attacks touched upon a highly sensitive nerve of the country's political culture: Its incessant search for giving unity to a deeply divided society. Since 1789, the country had for over more than two centuries continuously striven to regain the unity it had lost, once the deep divisions over the Revolution's objectives had broken up. The highly centralized state structure of France is a manifestation of this search, as it is often seen as the only guarantee against centrifugal tendencies, which would immediately come up as soon as the state would loosen its grip on society. However, moments of national unity have been extremely rare in France's recent history. Collective memory recollects especially three of them: The "sacred unity" of the summer of 1914, the armistice of November 11th 1918, and the liberation of Paris in August 1944. Thus, the wake of the terrorist attacks of 2015 meant for many French - along with the grief over the death of assassinated journalists, police, and citizens - the promise of a new, history-making moment of national unity. At first sight, January 11th strikingly resembled those seminal events of the 20th century. Since August 26th 1944, when more than half of the Parisians went to the streets in order to celebrate with Charles de Gaulle the liberation of the capital, there had never again been such a massive gathering of the population. And when the deputies of the National Assembly spontaneously sung "La Marseillaise", interrupting a minute of silence for the victims, it was for the first time since 1918 that the national anthem resounded in the hemicycle of Palais Bourbon.

The emotions accompanying these powerful symbols at first overshadowed the question to which extent the unity demonstrated in the aftermath of the shootings was really embracing the whole nation: Were actually all spiritual currents of France *Charlie*? Were the citizens who demonstrated on January 11th representative of the whole French population? Clearly the answer was 'no'. The fact that by far not all French had been or were *Charlie* became visible, when a significant number of pupils refused to observe a minute of silence for the killed journalists, ordered by the Minis-

---

6 Full text of Hollande's speech from 9 January 2015 on: http://www.elysee.fr/declara tions/article/adresse-a-la-nation-a-la-suite-des-evenements-des-7-et-8-janvier-2/.

ter of Education.[7] Also, it seemed conspicuous to observers that not many inhabitants of immigrant-dominated disadvantaged neighbourhoods had participated in the demonstrations of January 11th.[8] Thus, had the national unity been only an illusion? Have the deep cleavages of French society remained untouched by the events? Before advancing a preliminary answer to these questions, I first analyse the points of view of those French who "were not *Charlie*". None of these different currents of opinion, this must be underlined, does in any way justify or defend the violence against the journalists. However, they don't adhere to the national unity as it was celebrated on January 11th.

The first approach refuses the identification with the victims, which the formula *Je suis Charlie* insinuates. In the wake of the shootings, several citizens have expressed their difficulties to identify with a journal whose approach to religion seems offensive to them. The tragic death of the journalists does not, according to those voices, posthumously legitimize their disrespectful attitude towards believers and vindicate their decision to publish cartoons of the prophet Mohammed. It is important to stress that this current of thought is not limited to French citizens of Islamic religion, but is shared also by Christians who empathise with the feelings of Muslims about the cartoons and thus refuse to join the chorus of *Charlie* solidarity.[9]

The second approach goes a lot farer in its refusal of the call to national unity. For activists around the *Parti des indigènes de la République*, an anti-colonialist movement born in 2005, the government simply exploited the anxieties around the terrorist attacks in order to mask the unchanged state-supported discrimination of immigrants, the rampant islamophobia and racism of French society behind a discourse of unanimity. The incessant invocation of Republican and Western values, according to them, leads to further deepen the cleavage between an affluent middle class and

---

7 Cf.: Pauline Verduzier, Caroline Beyer, Charlie Hebdo: Ces minutes de silence qui ont dérapé dans les écoles, in: Le Figaro, 9/01/2015. http://www.lefigaro.fr/actualite-france/2015/01/09/01016-20150109ARTFIG00338-ces-minutes-de-silence-qui-ont-derape-dans-les-ecoles.php.

8 Cf.: Sylvia Zappi, La banlieu tiraillée entre "Charlie" et "pas Charlie", in: Le Monde, 16/01/2015, p. 4.

9 Cf.: Ahmed Jaballah, Certains usages de la liberté d'expression sont offensants, in: Le Monde, 16/01/2015, p. 10. Thibaud Collin, L'hebdo satirique n'est pas la France, in: Le Monde, 16/01/2015, p. 11.

an increasingly alienated, disenfranchised immigrant population.[10] They remind of the fact that Muslim minorities remain the most fragile ones in terms of educational and professional opportunities, as well as the most exposed to racist violence, demonstrated by the profanation of Mosques in the wake of the Charlie Hebdo attacks.

Closely related to these arguments is the third approach, which focuses on the international arena as a background for the killings.[11] For critics of French foreign policy, the country remains an imperialist power, which is not particularly considerate about human lives when intervening abroad, especially in the "war on terror" which President Hollande has declared in the Sahel zone.[12] The Charlie Hebdo attacks appear in this reading as a response to violence inflicted on Muslims through French power projection abroad. Such voices echo the famous reaction by Malcolm X on the killing of John F. Kennedy, when he said that "the chickens have come home to roost"[13]: Who sows violence should not be surprised if it strikes back one day.

The fourth approach, finally, draws on the contradictions of the French attitude towards the freedom of speech. This fundamental right is in France not as unrestricted as the many eulogies on Republican values in the wake of the Charlie Hebdo attacks have made it appear. In fact, contrary to the United States, France espouses a strictly framed attitude to the freedom of speech, penalizing such forms of expression considered as racial discrimination, defamation, support of terrorism or denial of the Holocaust. On the contrary, blasphemy, as it was practiced by Charlie Hebdo, received the blessing of the highest courts. The French authorities provided a telling example of their ambiguous attitude to the freedom of

---

10 Exemplary for this point of view: Said Bouamama, L'attentat contre Charlie Hebdo: L'occultation politique et médiatique des causes, des conséquences et des enjeux, 11/01/2015. http://indigenes-republique.fr/lattentat-contre-charlie-hebdo-locc ultation-politique-et-mediatique-des-causes-des-consequences-et-des-enjeux/.

11 Cf.: "Non à l'«union nationale» derrière les impérialistes! Oui à l'«union politique» antiraciste et anti-impérialiste!" Statement by the Parti des Indigènes de la République from 10/01/2015. http://indigenes-republique.fr/non-a-l-union-national e-derriere-les-imperialistes-oui-a-l-union-politique-antiraciste-et-anti-imperialiste/.

12 Cf.: "La 'guerre contre le terrorisme', version française," in: Le Monde, 15/01/2013. http://www.lemonde.fr/afrique/article/2013/01/15/la-guerre-contre-le-terrorisme-version-francaise_1817070_3212.html.

13 Malcolm X's comment on Kennedy's shooting on: https://www.youtube.com/watc h?v=SzuOOshpddM.

speech immediately after the terrorist attacks. The highly contested comedian Dieudonné published, after the hijacking of the cosher supermarket and the killing of four customers by Amedy Coulibaly, a post on his Facebook page: "Tonight I feel like Charlie Coulibaly". The public prosecutors started an inquiry against him for justification of terrorist acts. Also, the satirical journal itself has a past of auto-censorship, when its well-known cartoonist Siné was sacked in 2008, after he had made an allegedly anti-semitic remark about the son of President Sarkozy. Such contradictions, both on the part of public authorities and the journal itself, made it difficult for some citizens to embrace the slogan *Je suis Charlie*.[14]

In conclusion, it is difficult to judge how much support those voices critical of the national unity find. Opinion polls around the Charlie Hebdo events have been rare and produced ambiguous results. According to a poll published by Paris Match on January 10th, an overwhelming 97 per cent of those questioned agreed with the necessity to unite when faced with a terrorist threat.[15] However, there is no real consensus about the issues at stake: 42 per cent of those questioned in a poll from January 18th declare not being favourable of the publishing of Mohammed cartoons, if this is considered offensive by fellow citizens.[16] According to a recent poll, 17 per cent of those questioned believe that the killings were manoeuvred by a conspiracy; 30 per cent think that Dieudonnés remarks on Coulibaly should be considered as "humour" and not be subject to prosecution.[17]

Thus, the reading of January 11th as a day of national unity needs to be reconsidered. It was an event combining two interrelated processes: On the one hand the skilful mastery of the domestic political arena through President Hollande, who found the right words about the attacks so that little space for contestation by his rivals was left. On the other hand the strong concernedness of parts of the French population, for whom some of

---

14 For this discussion see: Rony Brauman, Le droit de l'outrance doit s'appliquer à tous, in: Le Monde, 15/01/2013, p.10.
15 Cf.: http://www.parismatch.com/Actu/Politique/Sondage-Charlie-Hebdo-97-des-F rancais-veulent-l-union-nationale-686944.
16 For the results of the poll see: http://www.metronews.fr/info/charlie-hebdo-sondag e-les-francais-partages-sur-la-publication-des-caricatures-et-la-limitation-de-la-lib erte-d-expression/moar!UZdrwLXBYXqnQ/.
17 Cf.: http://www.atlantico.fr/decryptage/17-francais-pensent-que-attentats-charlie-h ebdo-et-porte-vincenne-releveraient-complot-thermometre-etat-societe-yves-marie -cann-1971963.html.

the terrorist's victims were not anonymous faces, but well-known public figures whose cartoons they had cherished. The political truce manoeuvred by Hollande and the massive mobilization of the population worked together to forge the image of a united nation, unanimously defending the same values.[18] But this image only concealed the unchanged, deep divisions within French society.

The search for reasons and adequate responses

The perpetrators of the Charlie Hebdo and the kosher supermarket killings were French citizens of immigrant background. It was thus not possible, as in the case of the September 11th attacks, to externalize the causes of the attacks and to search for adequate responses in a war against "rogue states" sheltering terrorism. Similar to the London subway attacks of 2005, whose perpetrators had been British citizens, the quest for reasons necessarily had to focus on the domestic socio-cultural situation. The frames of the discussion were set almost immediately after the identity of the Charlie Hebdo killers, the brothers Said and Cherif Kouachi, was known. Without even a vague knowledge of their biographies, the public debate had already given a stereotypical image to the perpetrators, second-generation immigrants of Algerian descent: Originating from disadvantaged neighbourhoods and deprived of educational opportunities, they had failed to internalize the values of French-style secularism and had thus become an easy prey for djihadist indoctrination. The fact that the Kouachi brother's biographies were quite uncommon, that they had spent an essential part of their youth not in a dismal suburb but in the idyllic Corrèze region, did not change the tone of the debate.[19] They immediately became a symbol for the failure of immigrant integration, as their acts were perceived as an attack on the core values of the French republic.

It is needless to say that the public debate on immigration as it was triggered by the Charlie Hebdo attacks is not the first around those issues.

---

18 The media played a strong part in conveying this image. See as an example the title of "Libération" from Monday 12th January: "Nous sommes un peuple".

19 On the lives of the Kouachi brothers: Marion van Renterghem, Les frères Kouachi: une jeunesse française, in: Le Monde, 12/02/2015. http://abonnes.lemon de.fr/societe/article/2015/02/12/les-freres-kouachi-une-jeunesse-francaise_457511 5_3224.html.

Like a recurrent syndrome, the immigration and integration issue periodically dominates public discourse in France, but then almost disappears from the headlines of the media. At each time, the debate tends to look on different aspects of the problem. After the 2005 riots in the *banlieues*, the discussion centred on questions of security, illegal immigration, urban planning and social justice. When President Sarkozy launched in 2009/10 a "grand debate about national identity", the focus was on the meaning of frenchness for today's society, the role of the country's symbols and the question of national pride. The current debate concentrates on the issue of secularism, for two interrelated reasons. Firstly, the terrorists had targeted not only a journal whose generous use of France's permissiveness towards blasphemy has made it into a symbol of *laicité,* but also four citizens because of their religious affiliation to Judaism. Secondly, secularism is at the core of the French integration model and stands for the set of values, which immigrants should espouse.

At the same time, *laicité* is a concept whose pertinence for today's society is far from being clear. Its origins are to be found in the turn of the 19th to the 20th century, when the protagonists of the Third Republic pushed back the societal influence of the Catholic Church, which fiercely combated the principles of the new order and wanted to preserve its impact especially in the educational sector. French-style secularism thus contained from its outset a never solved ambiguity: On the one hand, it is a legal system, guaranteeing the neutrality of the state towards any religions and the freedom to practise them. On the other hand, it is a moral system, postulating a set of values, which should be transmitted by state-run education and which all citizens should embrace. Hence, *laicité* is a Janus-faced phenomenon, which can be tolerant (in its neutrality towards all religions) and intolerant (if citizens refuse to imbibe secular values) at the same time. Its merits for 20th century French society are incontestable: While the Catholic church succeeded in slowly accommodating to it, minority religions like Protestantism and Judaism were strongly attracted by it, because it provided them with the necessary space for their free development. New and unsolved problems for French-style secularism have come with the increased presence of Muslims: First, because it is a multifaceted and diverse religious community lacking an institutionalised representation (regardless of the attempts of the state to create one) and a unified position towards *laicité*. Second, the state's position towards the expression of Muslim faith in the public is sometimes perceived as intolerant, for example when it prohibits the veil in public schools or the niqab in the public space in general. Thus, some Muslims get the impression as if French-style secularism aimed at making them progressively abandon their faith in the process of their integration into the Republic. At the same time, some staunch advocates of *laïcité* clearly see Islam as a threat, since they fear it could partially reverse an advanced process of secularisation of society. However, as reminds us the historian and sociologist Jean Baubérot, *laïcité* and secularisation are two very different phenomena, which should not be mixed up.[20]

In the wake of the Charlie Hebdo attacks, the question of the pertinence of French-style secularism for the society of the 21st century has not been asked with the necessary consequence. Faced with the atrocities committed by the Kouachi brothers, many voices have taken a defensive position: "More *laïcité*" was their answer rather than "A different *laïcité*".[21] Also, the debate remains in a predominantly French frame of reference, as if secularism was still an element of the *exception française* and could be discussed without looking beyond one's own borders. At the beginning of the 20th century, France was clearly at the vanguard in terms of liberating civil society from constraints and implementing the religious neutrality of the state. Since then, many countries have invented their own models of secularism and have succeeded in accommodating highly diverse populations. Unfortunately, examples from other countries are rarely taken seriously in France, but are quickly disregarded as not pertinent to the French Republican model.[22] The multiculturalist integration model, which allows each sociocultural grouping to freely develop its distinctive features, is often perceived as necessarily leading to "communitarianism". This buzzword of French political discourse indicates a society divided into self-referential sociocultural groups, with only little connection in between

---

20 His most recent book among his prolific work on French laïcité is: La laïcité falsifiée, Paris 2014. See also his highly instructive blog on the site Mediapart: http://blogs.mediapart.fr/blog/jean-bauberot.

21 Exemplary for this defensive approach the speech by Manuel Valls in the National Assembly from 13/01/2015: "La laïcité ! La laïcité ! La laïcité, parce que c'est le cœur de la République et donc de l'école." http://www.gouvernement.fr/partage/31 18-seance-speciale-d-hommage-aux-victimes-des-attentats-allocution-de-manuel-v alls-premier-ministre.

22 Certainly there are exceptions to this generally unreceptive attitude towards foreign examples. See for instance: Arnaud Leparmentier, Questions sur la laïcité, in: Le Monde, 15/01/205, p. 23. Alain Renaut, La France doit faire le choix d'un multiculturalisme tempéré, in: Le Monde, 15/01/2015, p. 9.

them, thus the contrary of the ideal of a Republican society in which individual citizens share the same values. However, as long as foreign examples are mostly denigrated and not seriously examined, France will hardly advance in its search for a more integrated society. Why not introduce the teaching of comparative religions in public schools, so that children lose their prejudices about other beliefs and learn to historicize their own? Why not consider policies of affirmative action, in order to provide minority citizens with better educational and professional opportunities? Why not officially recognize the fact that France consists of different, linguistically, religiously and culturally defined groups, instead of insisting on homogeneity, which is less than ever attainable?

Possible electoral consequences

Profoundly shaking events like the terrorist attacks and the ensuing demonstration of national union will necessarily have their impact on the electoral landscape of France. Who will be able to take advantage of them, and which forces will be weakened? At first, the forcefully demonstrated unanimity of the centre right and left somewhat marginalized the Front National, whose leader Marine Le Pen acted awkwardly when demanding an explicit invitation to take part in the January 11th demonstration. The dominant public discourse around the events emphasized Republican values, instead of focusing on those themes, which are the stronghold of the Front National: security, toughness on criminal immigrants, strong protection of borders. However, several indicators show that the events have had little impact on the intention of many French citizens to vote for Front National. In the by-elections in the department of Doubs on February 1st and 8th, the FN candidate won the first round with 32,8 per cent and was defeated in the second round by a slight margin of some 900 votes. According to opinion polls carried out after the events, Marine Le Pen would be the frontrunner of the first round of the next presidential elections with roughly 30 per cent of those questioned currently intending to vote for her.[23] Thus, the republican unity of January 11th has not stopped the as-

---

23 Matthieu Goar, Marine Le Pen en tête, des sondages à lire avec prudence, in: Le Monde, 30/01/2015. http://www.lemonde.fr/politique/article/2015/01/30/marine-le -pen-en-tete-en-2017-des-sondages-a-lire-avec-prudence_4567091_823448.html.

cendancy of the Front National, whose leader has best chances to qualify for the second round of the next presidential elections.

Meanwhile, President Hollande has seen his position strengthened by the Charlie Hebdo events. The pivotal problem of his presidency so far had been that the French massively questioned his clout to live up to the challenges of his office and to provide guidance to the country. His impeccable attitude in the days of the terrorist attacks has lifted many doubts about his capacity for leadership. Hence, his re-election in 2017, which seemed totally out of reach before the Charlie Hebdo events, has now become a serious option.

It is the centre-right UMP that has not been able to capitalize on the events. In fact, the deep internal contradictions of the party led by ex-president Sarkozy have become more apparent with the by-elections in the department of Doubs: The UMP candidate scored only third and could not qualify for the second round. The party leaders deeply disagree about which position to take in the case of a second election round between a Socialist and a Front National candidate, whether to opt for a "republican front" and support the socialist or to remain neutral and thus risk the victory of the Front National. As to its political agenda, the party is lacking a unifying, mobilising theme. If it takes a tough stance on immigration, Islam, and security, it risks alienating moderate voters, while not being sufficiently attractive for right-wingers, who tend to prefer the original (Front National) rather than the copy (UMP). The Socialist government having opted for a supply-side economic policy, the centre right finds it difficult to propose a different approach to the problems of growth, unemployment and public debt. It seems that more and more voters see in Front National the real alternative to the government in place.

(published online mid-February 2015)

The UK's Block-Opt-Out – Serious Effects or Yet Another Peculiarity in EU-UK Relations?

Funda Tekin

On December 1st the pre-Lisbon Treaty 3rd pillar acquis on police and judicial cooperation in criminal matters ceases to apply to the United Kingdom (UK). These days in which the EU is challenged by crises such as in the Ukraine or moved by institutional reforms such as the newly structured European Commission, this so-called ,block-opt-out' of the UK risks to take effect rather unnoticed. Yet, given the densely interrelated measures within police and judicial cooperation in criminal matters and the entire Area of Freedom, Security and Justice (AFSJ) it is important to assess the implications of this opt-out. Will there be substantial effects on coherence and operability within policing and criminal law or can this merely be perceived as yet another peculiarity in EU-UK relations? This question shall be answered in light of differentiated integration and its effects in the AFSJ.

Differentiated Integration in the Area of Freedom, Security and Justice: Cherry-Picking at its Best?

Differentiated integration in the AFSJ including the Schengen acquis is of highly volatile nature. Other than in other policy areas subject to forms of pre-defined differentiation (e.g. the Euro) where you can clearly distinguish those Member States participating from those Member States with a derogation in the AFJS the UK, Ireland and Denmark have the right to decide on an ad hoc basis whether to participate in individual policy measures. It is often claimed that this cherry-picking option allows these three Member States to 'get the best of both worlds'. However, the highly complex legal procedures for opting-in and –out have inbuilt provisions that aim at preserving both the coherence and the operability of the AFSJ acquis. The basic principle that counts is 'once you are in you remain in and once you are out you remain out'. This produces mechanisms of so-called 'opt-in/opt-out spill-overs' by which the UK, Ireland and Denmark will be required or urged to participate in a measure that is closely linked to a measure of which they form already part and vice versa. The aim is to subordinate the freedom of choice to the coherence and operability of the AFSJ acquis.

Block-Opt-Out: What is It?

Prior to the Lisbon Treaty police and judicial cooperation in criminal matters formed the 3rd pillar acquis. This implied that it was subject to intergovernmental decision-making. Thus, differentiated integration of the pre-Lisbon Treaty era did not include 3rd pillar legislation except for the Schengen-based measures because neither the UK nor Ireland have signed the Schengen Agreement. Instead, the UK, Ireland and Denmark were entitled to a veto. Additionally, the competences of both the European Commission and the Court of Justice of the European Union (CJEU) were limited. The Lisbon Treaty abolished the pillar structure altogether implying the communitarisation of the policing and criminal justice legal procedures and acquis. Yet, Article 10 of Protocol 36 annexed to the Lisbon Treaty defined a transitional period of five years before the full powers of the Commission and the CJEU were to take effect regarding the 130 acts adopted before the entry into force of the Lisbon Treaty. Only from 1 December 2014 onwards the Commission as the guardian of the treaties shall have the right to bring infringement procedures against Member States to the CJEU and the CJEU shall have full jurisdiction including proceedings for a preliminary ruling. The UK negotiated the extension of the opt-out/opt-in procedures to the police and judicial cooperation in criminal matters. Additionally, Article 10 of Protocol 36 defines the UK's right to decide by June 2014 the latest whether or not the full powers of the Commission and the CJEU will be acceptable regarding the pre-Lisbon acquis in this policy area. In case of rejecting these powers the relevant measures will cease to be applicable to the UK with the end of the transitional period. The Council without the participation of the UK will determine the necessary consequential and transitional arrangements including potential financial consequences that the UK will be obliged to bear.

The UK notified the Council of the decision to implement this block-opt-out already in 2013.[1] At the same time it wishes to make use of the option provided by Article 10 of Protocol 36 to opt-back-in to measures that are subject to this block-opt-out. A list of 35 measures[2] was presented and has been informally negotiated with the Council and the Commission. However, this opt-out and opt-back-in is subject to a clear-cut two-step approach. The block-opt-out will take effect on 1 December 2014 and the decision on the opt-back-in will be subject to the general opt-out/opt-in procedures applicable to the UK in the AFSJ and taken only afterwards – by the Council regarding Schengen-based measures and by the Commission regarding the remaining acts. This implies that for the time being the UK will not apply under EU law the acts of police and judicial cooperation in criminal matters that were adopted prior to the Lisbon Treaty.

Block-Opt-Out: What is at Stake?

In terms of 'differentiated integration at work' i.e. the implementation of legal opt-out or opt-in rights two aspects need consideration regarding the UK's block-opt-out. First, Article 10 of Protocol 36 gives yet again special treatment to the UK. Second, the coherence and operability of the policing and criminal justice acquis might be substantially affected.

1. On the special treatment of the UK: The five years transitional period for the full powers of the Commission and the CJEU is applicable to all EU Member States except for the UK and Denmark. The latter represents a special case of participation in the AFSJ under the Lisbon Treaty. Denmark is not prepared to participate in the AFSJ other than subject to intergovernmental cooperation. Given the full communitarisation of this acquis by the Lisbon Treaty, Denmark has the right to apply the acts adopted in the field of police and judicial cooperation in criminal matters before the entering into force of the Lisbon Treaty "unchanged" (Art. 2, Protocol 22). The UK on the other hand negotiat-

---

1 For considerations on this decision see Stephen Booth, Christopher Howarth and Vincenzo Scarpetta: An unavoidable choice: More or less EU control over UK policing and criminal law, open europe, January 2012.
2 Decision persuant to Article 10 of Protocol 36 to The Treaty on the Functioning of the European Union, presented to Parliament by the Secretary of State for the Home Department by Command of her Majesty, July 2013.

ed the block-opt-out including the right to determine the scope of its participation by cherry-picking the acts of interest afterwards. Set aside the fact that this block-opt-out only adds to the already existing substantial opt-out and opt-in rights extending the privileged position of the UK, two aspects might actually strain the patience of the other EU Member States. The announcement of the referendum on the EU membership of the UK in 2017 combined with the plans to negotiate the repatriation of competences puts the legal certainty of the UK opt-in position in police and judicial cooperation in criminal matters at stake. Additionally, the UK has combined opt-in ambitions with requests to amend certain rules – e.g. the UK requests to include a form of proportionality assessment for the transmission of European Arrest Warrants (EAW) through the Schengen Information System (SIS II). Such a conditional opt-in combined with the general ambition to repatriate competences is not well perceived by the other EU Member States.[3]

2. On the coherence and operability of the policing and criminal justice acquis: In general the volatility of British participation in police and judicial cooperation in criminal matters due to the opt-out and opt-in rights including the block-opt-out does not represent a problem. The coherence and operability of the policing and criminal justice area will not be severely affected if the UK decides to refrain from the application of certain standards or individual measures. The case is different, however, if systems of mutual recognition are directly or indirectly concerned. Equal participation in the EAW for instance can only be provided if the UK is also prepared to apply the Directives on access to a lawyer, translation and interpretation and the right to information in criminal procedures. This means that great attention will have to be paid to allow for the mechanisms of opt-in/opt-out spill-over taking effect. To this end the list of the 35 acts that the UK wishes to opt-back-in is thoroughly assessed by the so-called 'Friends of the Presidency Group'. This list includes the main features of the police and judicial cooperation in criminal matters such as the EAW, the Schengen-based police cooperation measures, Europol and Eurojust. With the aim to ensure coherence and operability of the policy area this list was extended to include Council Decisions implementing the Europol Deci-

---

3 Steve Peers: The UK opt-out from Justice and Home Affairs law: the other Member States finally lose patience, statewatch analysis, 26 March 2014.

sion and establishing the European Judicial Network. Furthermore, since the list excluded the so-called Prüm Decisions on cross-border exchange of information on DNA, licence plate information and fingerprints, the Council defined financial consequences linked to this non-participation amounting to some 1.5 Mio Euros that the UK will have to bear if it does not opt-back-in to Prüm in the near future[4]. Finally, the scope of the opt-back-in might change over time given the continued so-called 'Lisbonisation' of the policing and criminal matters acquis in terms of the amendment, replacement or repeal of pre-Lisbon 3rd pillar acts under the Lisbon Treaty. The UK has opted-in to the acts that have been amended or replaced so far reducing the scope of the block-opt-out. Provisions on Eurojust and Europol are very likely to be subject to the Lisbonisation procedure next, which will question the UK's continued participation. On the one hand, the UK will be obliged to officially opt-in again if the interest to participate remains. On the other hand the Commission will have the opportunity to verify the operability and coherence of the acquis when it decides on the UK's opt-in request.

Conclusions

Without doubt the block-opt-out represents an extreme form of volatility in the AFSJ adding to the complexity and scope of the already existing opt-in and opt-out rights of the UK. However, the UK is the only country that is entitled to this procedure. Therefore, it is very unlikely that the police and judicial cooperation in criminal matters risks to disintegrate into variable geometries as is suspected by some studies[5]. Nevertheless, the UK's cherry-picking might jeopardise the coherence and operability of the

---

4 Council Decision 14018/14 determining certain direct financial consequences incurred as a result of the cessation of the participation of the United Kingdom of Great Britain and Northern Ireland in certain acts of the Union in the field of police and judicial cooperation in criminal matters adopted before the entry into force of the Lisbon Treaty, 09. Oktober 2014.
5 Valsamis Mitsilegas, Sergio Carrera and Katharina Eisele: The End of the Transitional Period for Police and Criminal Justice Measures Adopted before the Lisbon Treaty. Who Monitors Trust in the European Justice Area?, Document requested by the Committee on Civil Liberties, Justice and Home Affairs, European Parliament, 2014.

police and judicial cooperation in criminal matters. In order to avoid this the legal provisions that allow for mechanisms of opt-in- /opt-out spill-over will have to take full effect and the legal certainty of the UK's partic-ipation will have to be granted.

(published online end of November 2014)

The new phase of the Greek drama

George N. Tzogopoulos

The Greek election of 26 January 2015 has brought the European debt crisis back to the international agenda. The victory of the leftist SY.RIZ.A party and its co-operation with the populist rightwing Independent Greeks one signal the beginning of a new, different period for Europe. The Greek government, which is unexperienced and unfamiliar with the modus operandi of the European Union, attempts to develop its own agenda risking to derail the international commitments of the country and arguably its European orientation.

From the very first beginning the Greek government was encountered with a serious dilemma. It either had to agree with bailout terms and ask for an extension of the current program which would expire by the end of February or become isolated and lose its access to liquidity[1]. The first weeks of February were dramatic. Greek Finance Minister Yanis Varoufakis attempted to convince his European partners including German Finance Minister Wolfgang Schäuble and his French counterpart Michel Sapin that previous rescue packages had been unsuccessful recommending subsequently a reconsideration of the European economic policy vis-à-vis Greece and a relaxation of terms. However, his effort proved unsuccessful. Wolfgang Schäuble reminded him during a meeting they had in Berlin on 5 February, for instance, that agreements have to be respected.[2] On the whole, Germany is not prepared to accept changes in a financing program which had been accepted by all Eurozone parliaments in the past and is currently in progress.

Within this context, the Eurogroup of 16 February 2015 handed over an ultimatum to the Greek government to request an extension of the current

---

1 George Tzogopoulos, 'Greece facing hard choice over debt issue', Xinhua, 6 February 2015, available at: http://news.xinhuanet.com/english/europe/europe/2015-02/0 7/c_133976221.htm [accessed March 2015]
2 Deutsche Welle, 'Varoufakis-Schäuble meeting draws sharp reactions', 6 February 2015, available at: http://www.dw.de/varoufakis-sch%C3%A4uble-meeting-draws-sharp-reactions/a-18241816 [accessed March 2015].

bailout.[3] Two days later Yanis Varoufakis sent a letter 'applying for the extension of the Master Financial Assistance Facility Agreement for a period of six months'[4]. The reaction of Germany was negative. Analysing the argumentation of Varoufakis, spokesman of Schäuble Martin Jäger regarded the proposal as a 'non substantial one' on 19 February[5]. In the next dramatic hours until the Eurogroup of the day after, the Greek government promised to remain committed to the country's obligations and proposed to present its own reform ideas to be assessed by the European Central Bank, the European Commission and the International Monetary Fund. On these grounds, an agreement was reached stipulating for an extension of the program for four months - instead of six [6].

During the ongoing crisis, it is an observable phenomenon that after winning an election, Greek politicians are brought back to harsh reality at once.[7] Pre-election promises, populism and illusions are buried when unavoidable decisions have to be made at the international level. In that regard, the Greek government's request for an extension of the bailout program is not surprising. Nonetheless, the difference between words and deeds is always large. Approximately four weeks after the Eurogroup's decision of 20 February, progress was rather poor. The Greek government found it hard to deliver domestically because many of its members and voters were expecting a strong anti-bailout course. Ironically, instead of immediately providing solutions to problems, SYRIZA has preferred to employ a different communication strategy in front of the international and the national audiences respectively.

---

3 EUbusiness, 'Greece handed ultimatum as Eurozone bailout talks collapse', 17 February 2015, available at: http://www.eubusiness.com/news-eu/greece-politics.z wa [accessed March 2015].

4 Reuters, 'TEXT-Greek request letter for bailout extension', 19 February 2015, available at: http://in.reuters.com/article/2015/02/19/eurozone-greece-request-idIN L5N0VT2S720150219 [accessed March 2015].

5 Deutsche Welle, 'Greece faces decisive round of finance negotiations, 20 February 2015, available at: http://www.dw.de/greece-faces-decisive-round-of-finance-nego-tiations/a-18270040 [accessed March 2015].

6 Eurogroup Statement on Greece, 20 February 2015, available at: http://www.consili um.europa.eu/en/press/press-releases/2015/02/150220-eurogroup-statement-greece/ [accessed March 2015.

7 George Tzogopoulos, 'Time for Greek government to face reality', Xinhua, 27 February 2015 http://news.xinhuanet.com/english/2015-02/27/c_134021697.htm [accessed March 2015.

Seeing the lack of progress and realising that the country is running out of cash, Greek Prime Minister Alexis Tsipras sent a letter to Chancellor Merkel on 15 March 2015. In this letter, he dramatically focused on his future dilemma of being forced to either pay for salaries and pensions or for Greece's international obligations[8]. He therefore asked for an understanding by the creditors of the country in safeguarding its liquidity. Five days later, on 20 March, Presidents of the European Council, the European Commission and the Eurogroup reconfirmed their adherence to Eurogroup's agreement of 20 February during a meeting with Premier Tsipras, Chanchellor Merkel and President Hollande in Brussels[9].

Although the Greek Prime Minister is endeavouring to provide a political dimension to the European negotiations of the Greek crisis, he has not managed to escape from the rule of supervision by the Institutions, previously known as Troika. Chancellor Angela Merkel focused on this critical aspect in a press conference following her conversation with the Greek Premier in Berlin on 23 March[10]. All in all, the Greek government can have the 'ownership of reforms' according to the afore-mentioned statement of 20 March but these reforms need to be evaluated by its creditors concerning their efficiency and fiscal impact.

Future developments remain unknown as they largely depend on the policies of the Greek government. The main challenge for it goes beyond submitting a satisfactory reform proposal to the Eurogroup. Important as it is, this proposal will only be valuable if SY.RIZ.A will practically deliver. For the time being European partners fail to trust it. That is because they have clarified that no disbursement of payment will be made before reforms start to be carried out. It is certainly not a positive sign that important European politicians including German Finance Minister Wolfgang Schäuble and European Commissioner Pierre Moscovici do not now pub-

---

8 Peter Spiegel, 'Tsipras letter to Merkel: the annotated text', 22 Match 2015, available at: http://blogs.ft.com/brusselsblog/2015/03/22/tsipras-letter-to-merkel-the-an notated-text/ [accessed March 2015, subscription required]

9 Statement by the Presidents of the European Council, the Commission and the Eurogroup on Greece, 20 March 2015, available at: http://europa.eu/rapid/press-relea se_STATEMENT-15-4642_en.htm [accessed March 2015]

10 Pressekonferenz von Bundeskanzlerin Merkel und dem griechischen Ministerpräsidenten Tsipras, 23 March 2015, available at: http://www.bundesregierung.de/Co ntent/DE/Mitschrift/Pressekonferenzen/2015/03/215-03-23-merkel-tsipras.html [accessed March 2015].

licly exclude a 'Grexit' for the first time since the outbreak of the debt crisis[11].

The mission of the new government is difficult. That is because it still seems to be a hostage of its own pre-election rhetoric and promises. Prime Minister Tsipras himself appears prepared to follow the path of realism and stop blaming external factors – mainly Germany – for Greece's problem. This is what he said in front of Chancellor Merkel for the first time in his political career[12]. It is now his responsibility to convince his party and the Independent Greeks on why he has decided to abandon his anti-German logic - which almost brought him to power - in a matter of hours.

Theoretically, SY.RIZ.A has now a unique opportunity. It can benefit from the existing flexibility of the bailout program and focus more on structural reforms than on austerity[13]. Experience from the administration of previous Greek governments suggests that they had not been prepared to efficiently fight against tax-evasion and corruption. SY.RIZ.A, which had not governed in the past, might possibly break the vicious circle. In parallel with this, Greek citizens who are frustrated with traditional parties – namely New Democracy and PA.SO.K – will possibly support a reform policy implemented by new figures and not old-guards, quasi professionals of the political landscape.

The current situation is critical though and does not allow much optimism. There are two sine qua non parameters the Greek government needs to accept in order to further proceed. The first is the need of a final conclusion of the ongoing bailout program under arranged terms. And the second is the commitment to continue fiscal consolidation and draw on balanced budgets. If the Greek government practically adapts to these requirements, its European partners will not withdraw their support. But if it ignores them, their patience will possibly expire. (published online end of March 2015)

---

11 ARD Tagesschau, 'Schäuble hält Grexit-Unfall für denkbar', 13 March 2015, available at: http://www.tagesschau.de/ausland/grexit-121.html [accessed March 2015] and Die Welt, 'Griechenland nicht zu jedem Preis im Euro halten', 18 March 2015, available at: http://www.welt.de/politik/deutschland/article13850519 8/Griechenland-nicht-zu-jedem-Preis-im-Euro-halten.html [accessed March 2015].

12 Pressekonferenz von Bundeskanzlerin Merkel und dem griechischen Ministerpräsidenten Tsipras, 23 March 2015.

13 See for example, George Tzogopoulos, 'SY.RIZ.A to fight media oligarchs', 31 January 2015, available at: http://en.ejo.ch/10127/media_politics/sy-riz-fight-medi a-oligarchs [accessed March 2015]

Looking behind the curtain: what about the Hungarian „economic miracle"?

András Inotai

In the last period, the Hungarian, and partly also the international media have been full of positive economic developments in Hungary. In fact, GDP grew by 3.6 per cent in 2014, the second highest among the EU-28 after Ireland. Also, for 2015 a growth of 3.2 per cent is forecast, almost the double of the EU-28 average. As a major achievement, after one decade starting with the accession in 2004, Hungary could leave the EU's excessive deficit procedure and produce a budget deficit below 3 per cent in 2014 (and most probably sustainable in 2015). This places the country in the middle-field of the new member countries and definitely into the frontline of all EU members, not least as compared to the Eurozone countries. Official unemployment rate has been continuously falling in the last years. Inflation is near zero, partly due to rapidly falling energy prices and constrained domestic demand. The prime interest rate set by the National Bank of Hungary reached historically low level. At the same time, trade and current account balances register large surplus, an important factor of (re)financing external debt. Also, not without some fluctuations, external debt between 76 and 80 per cent, the highest among the new member countries excepting Croatia, shows a declining path, and the burden of refinancing has been eased in the last year. Finally, after a rather long period of hesitation, Moody's has partially upgraded Hungary by changing the negative outlook to stable, but without taking out Hungary of the category of countries not recommended for investors.

On the other hand, most of the internationally recognized institutions seem to be much less convinced of the „miracle" in general, and its sustainability, in particular. It is a justified question, why international credit rating agencies remain untouched by the obviously positive economic developments in Hungary and as of today have been delaying any meaningful upgrading. More importantly, Hungary's position in different international comparisons has worsened. The World Bank's Doing Business ranking puts Hungary on place 54 (among 189 countries), but just on place 128 concerning the protection of investments. Concerning the Happiness indicator, Hungary reached place 110, among 156 countries. In international competitiveness, as reported in the annual Global Competitiveness Report, the decline is alarming, from place 48 (among 148 countries) in 2011 to place 63 in 2015. Moreover, the recently published Sustainable Governance Indicator report containing relevant data on the 41 OECD countries and regularly published by the Bertelsmann Foundation puts Hungary on place 41 concerning democracy, place 35 in policy performance (within it rank 38 for economic and rank 39 for social policies) and place 38 in governance (including rank 40 in executive accountability). In addition, the latest report (April 2015) of the German-Hungarian Chamber of Industry and Commerce did not recognize the „miraculous" macroeconomic performance of Hungary either. In regional comparison, the country remains in the (lower) middle-field, business confidence is lacking, and several German companies would not come again to Hungary or, if already here, would not consider to make further investments, due to serious restrictions and higher taxes in most service sector areas (banking, telecommunications, public utilities, retail trade). Claims about corruption, intransparency, uncalculable policy measures can be heard and read almost every day.

How can this discrepancy be explained? Has the Hungarian government after 2010 really created a „miracle" based on its often publicized „unorthodox economic policy"? And if yes, to what extent is it sustainable, and which have been and most probably will be the costs of the „miracle"? This personal survey is a strictly economic one, although the author is fully aware of the political, social and psychological roots and (potential) consequences of „miracle-making". However, the analysis of these interdependences should be the topic of another and longer study.

1. Factors of GDP growth

Before going into details, it has to be stated that – despite the 3.6 per cent growth in 2014 – Hungary still did not reach the pre-crisis (2008) output level. While Poland indicated a 17 per cent and Slovakia an 8 per cent cumulative GDP growth between 2008 and 2014, Hungary's figure was 98 (and the Czech Republic's 99). Among the factors of GDP growth, exports proved to be the key engine of growth, while domestic consumption represented a modest growth and investments still could not recover from the dramatic decline after 2008 and further deteriorated by anti-capital „freedom fighting" of the government after 2010. As compared to neighbouring countries, the growth of Hungarian exports (10 per cent between 2008 and 2013) was lagging behind the respective Slovak (34 %), Polish (31 %) and Czech (22 %) figures. Even in the leading Hungarian export market, which is Germany, Hungary's relative position has been weakened vis-a-vis Poland and the Czech Republic. Export-driven growth was increasingly characterized by structural deformation caused by the unilateral concentration on car manufacturing (new Mercedes plant, Audi, Suzuki). As a result, the previously well diversified export structure started to resemble the late-comer Slovak „pattern", not only embedding higher vulnerability in case of any future crisis but also largely exposed to the next wave of Chinese export drive to Europe which will definitely include the not yet challenged European car market.

Similar to other EU members, but with a politics-driven communication campaign, in 2012 the Hungarian government announced its „opening to the East" policy. The underlying argument was correct: if the EU markets are stagnating and a small and open, export-driven economy needs growing markets, a turn to extra-EU opportunities, mainly offered by emerging and rapidly developing countries is justified. However, for several reasons, and despite nebulous commitments, the Hungarian policy proved to be less successful. Between 2008 and 2013 the intra-EU share of the EU-28 in EU-exports fell from 67 to 62 per cent, a clear sign of geographic reorientation without denying the priority of the EU markets. In Hungary, the change resulted in a shift from 78 to 76 per cent of intra-EU and from 22 to 24 per cent of extra-EU exports. In other neighbouring countries, without any politically and ideologically motivated campaign, this shift was more successful. As a clear proof of failure, Hungary's exports to Asia amounted to 6.6 per cent of total exports in 2011 and to just 5 per cent in 2014. More successful proved to be the opening up to the East in imports. Definitely not in imports of commodities, but of anti-democratic, anti-Western, anti-EU „values". Most recently, a new „opening to the South" (Africa and Latin America) was announced, with a total share of 2.1 per cent in Hungarian exports. For this purpose, a number of Hungarian „trading houses" will be established in selected countries, without any knowledge of markets and exportable commodities but with quite convenient jobs for close friends of the government. It has to be mentioned that Hungary's exports outside the EU are dominated by goods produced by transnational companies in Hungary (e.g. 90 per cent of exports to China).

Or, commodities made in Hungary are first exported to Germany and contribute to German exports to third countries.

As a second factor of explaining GDP growth, domestic consumption has modestly recovered in the last two years. A 4 per cent income increase accompanied by almost no-inflation mainly generated by the halving of oil prices was one factor. However, there have been several other components of higher domestic demand which can hardly be sustained in the future.

First, mainly for domestic political reasons (before the parliamentary elections of 2014) the government reduced the utility prices for private consumers (electricity, heating, water) in order to leave more money with the households. Similar to the introduction of the flat tax on personal income in 2011, again without considering justified social redistribution aspects, to make a difference between small and large-scale consumers (e.g. those who have a large house and used to heat their swimming pool). The potential and very likely consequences of lower revenues have already had negative impact on utility providers who, in the future, will hardly be able to finance even the most important maintenance investments. Moreover, the additional costs of nationalizing previously internationally-led public utility companies (very much according to the logic of „freedom fighting") remained ignored by the decision-making politicians.

Second, many Hungarian households have been bailed-out of the Swiss Franc denominated debt trap at an exchange rate of HUF 256 against CHF 1 before Switzerland abandoned its Euro-linked exchange rate policy in January 2015. However, previously many politicians (from different parties) were given the possibility to make the same conversion at an exchange rate of HUF 180 to 1 CHF. It has to be added that the bail-out project cost about 2 bn Euro for the banking sector and had to be financed by official reserves of the National Bank of Hungary. Finally, many bailed-out persons expected much better terms of continuing debt-financing in Hungarian forints than their new accounts indicate.

Third, the historically low level of interest rate on traditional savings (considering the bank costs, practically zero or negative interest rates) initiated a massive outflow of money both into Euro (capital flight) and to alternative investments, such as housing (housing prices grew by 20 per cent in the last years), durable consumer goods, government bonds and stock exchange. At least in the two latter cases not without risk well beyond the financial sphere.

Low level of investment activities is the most critical point of the „miracle". In fact, investment activities are still far below the 2008 figures despite the spectacular increase of mainly EU-financed public investments. Excluding some large private sector investments in the car industry based on agreements signed before 2010 (Mercedes, Audi), private investments are almost non-existent. The lack of investments due to the loss of confidence of both foreign and domestic potential investors, is seriously jeopardizing the sustainability of competitiveness, since small but continuous „modernization investments" would be necessary to permanent upgrading of competitive production and service activities. Interestingly, continuously declining interes rates were not able to generate massive new investments. Indeed, indebted private companies made broad use of the National Bank's offer to change higher-interest rate debts into lower-interest rate debts. However, it did not launch a new wave of investments, due to prevailing legal and economic uncertainty and the reluctance of most banks to lend money while being forced to consolidate their own budget after various haircuts suffered by „unorthodox" government measures.

In sum, the Hungarian „growth miracle" seems to be unsustainable for several reasons.

First, in 2014 agriculture (with about 5 per cent of GDP) reported record output which cannot be repeated this year (latest figures anticipate an almost two-digit decline as compared to 2014).

Second, the car industry (mainly the so-called Mercedes impact) is about to reach its peak performance (working in three shifts around the clock). Other industrial sectors as potential future drivers of manufacturing growth cannot yet be identified.

Third, and most importantly, EU money has been the key engine of the „miraculous" growth between 2013 and 2015. In the Multiannual Financial Framework (MFF) covering the period between 2007 and 2013 Hungary was entitled to have access to about Euro 23 bn, or more than Euro 3 bn a year. Out of this sum, annually about Euro 1 bn has to be deducted due to the Hungarian contribution to the common budget. In contrast, this transfer does not include direct payments to farmers (Common Agricultural Policy) in the amount of Euro 1.5 bn annually and several other payments outside the cohesion fund. Since the available money has not been used evenly across the seven year period, due both to budgetary rules (application, long preparatory periods) and to the negligent attitude of the Hungarian government after the political change in 2010, characterized by institutional uncertainties about who is really entitled to manage the EU funds, a large part of the available money had to be used in the last three years (from 2013 to 2015, being 2015 the last year of having access to funds of the 2007-2013 MFF period). In consequence, as of 2013, the government started to make a lot of attempts at getting the most of the money, without any consideration of its longer-term multiplier effects. Still, it can be assumed that on the average of 2013-2015, more than the annual amount of Euro 3 bn has arrived. This represents almost 3 per cent of the Hungarian GDP. In other words, just the inflow of the EU transfers could produce a statistical growth rate of 3 per cent. However, this „honeymoon" period will be over at the end of 2015. Of course, a new transfer channel is already opened within the MFF 2014-2020, but access to money will need a longer period of preparation. Therefore, new money will start flowing slowly and will certainly remain below average (still about Euro 3 bn annually) at least in 2016 and probably also in 2017. In addition, several rules of the game have been changed and instead of a one-way support, the financing of most projects will need domestic co-financing, with clear implication on the budgetary expenses if Hungary wants to keep on having access to EU funds. Moreover, the government has to be prepared to a two-way flow of money, because, at present, several procedures and investigations initiated by Brussels are in process, and more are expected to come due to Hungarian policy measures that violate several basic EU rules of competition (from retail trade through energy to various services). Not less important impacts, with repayment obligation may be expected from the already ongoing anti-fraud (anti-corruption) investigation by OLAF concerning several projects financed by EU money. In sum, it is not unlikely that the net transfer of EU money to Hungary in 2016 will be near to zero. Therefore, the key elements of the „economic miracle" are likely to be substantially reduced or even disappearing, with the most serious consequences on construction and partly public work, since both areas have almost exclusively been financed from EU funds. Also, the small- and medium sized entrepreneurial sector could be seriously hit, since, between 2007 and 2013, about 80 per cent of its total external financing has arrived from EU transfers. The only exception will be the continuous flow of direct support to agriculture, which has become a key political and financial issue for the current government how to put close friends into the position of new landowners.

2. Reduction of budget deficit

At first sight, the reduction of budget deficit below 3 per cent of the GDP seems to be a success story. However, the way in which it has been implemented, has not only questioned the sustainability of the „miracle" but has undermined the medium- and longer-term growth prospects of Hungary.

First, one of the first measures of the „unorthodox" economic policy was the imposition of special and several times discriminatory taxes on selected sectors, mainly dominated by foreign companies (energy, telecommunications, retail trade, banking). Although, for various reasons, most of the affected firms remained in Hungary, they stopped or seriously cut their planned investments, with negative impact on future growth and job creation. In addition, several legal processes are on the way because companies have indicted the government at the respective EU bodies on violating basic rules of competition. Some jugdements are already known, obliging the Hungarian authorities to restore conditions of competitiveness and/or paying indemnization. Many others are likely to follow. Moreover, the government once having come to power promised the simplification of the tax system. In contrast, in the last years not less than about 70 new taxes have been introduced, most of them making normal business more complicated or even making investments impossible.

Second, as one of the first steps which would have been unimaginable in any democratic country, the government, at one strike, nationalized (in better terms „bolshevized") the private pension funds representing Euro 11 bn (or 10 per cent of the Hungarian GDP) in 2011. For there was no massive protest by 3 million people involved in this scheme (a topic that throws light on one of the most important non-economic factors of „economic miracle"), the government correctly calculated that if such a measure does not provoke resistance, practically everything can be done as long as it is at power. Up to today, we do not know what has happened with this money. Most probably, part has been used for budgetary consolidation and another part to reduce – with very ambiguous results – the external debt. We do not know whether some money is still available for future budget consolidation.

Third, dramatic cuts have been implemented in the expenditure side of the budget. On the one hand, the gap generated by the introduction of the flat income tax (economically irrational and socially immoral) has caused a budgetary revenue fall by about Euro 2 bn. This gap had to be filled by other incomes and by special savings. Beyond a number of areas cutting social welfare payments and unemployment benefits, both leading to increasing poverty and growing income and social gap within the Hungarian population, the farthest-reaching negative consequences can be identified in the dramatically underfinanced healthcare and educational system. Budgetary support for both of them has been cut from year to year, and the 2016 budget includes just these two items with declining budgetary support (even in nominal terms), namely healthcare and education (against a dramatic rise of budgetary support for police and antiterrorist activities). Moreover, education has been practically nationalized and the obligatory period of learning reduced to 16 years – in order to create a large amount of unskilled workers who, as the government believes, fit into and can be adjusted to a „modern slavery system", a desired background of and support to a long-term authoritarian regime. Instead of increasing the number of university students, several disciplines have been cancelled (e.g. international relations), renowned universities are planned to be split and reorganized. In sum, the human resource basis of the country, the fundamental medium- and longer-term factor of sustainable development and international competitiveness is dramatically threatened.

3. Labour market, unemployment

Again, at first glance, the labour market reveals one positive development. According to official statistics, previously double-digit unemployment rate has come down to 7 per cent, while long-term and structural unemployment remains high and the activity rate of the population is still at 67 %, below the EU-28 average (72.3 %), let alone the Czech Republic (73.5), Austria (75.4) or Germany (77.7).

At a closer look, the „employment miracle" reflects the classic way of deliberate mis-communication of the government.

First, employment data include also most Hungarian citizens who are working abroad. Their number has skyrocketed in the last five years and reached about 400 to 500 thousand persons (about 4-5 per cent of the population and 7 to 9 per cent of the active population). It is twice as much as the number of emigrants after the 1956 revolution. In fact, for decades, Hungary has not been an emigration country (like Poland, ex-Yugoslavia or the Baltics). Even after the 2004 accession to the EU outflow of Hungarian labour remained modest and concentrated on higher-skilled sectors (computer engineering in Ireland and the United Kingdom, doctors in

Sweden) or focused on commuting in border-near Austrian regions. The dramatic turn-around occurred after 2010 and can hardly be attributed just to economic reasons. Namely, wage differences between Hungary and the old EU member countries existed from the very beginning, and, maybe, in some sectors they have been narrowed in the first decade of EU membership. The unanimous driving motive of going out of the country were the increasingly suffocating political and human climate and the growing sense of apathy, frustration and hopelessness. As a consequence, already today, we can experience a lack of skilled workers in many sectors. Already in the near future, this may become one of the major obstacles of attracting foreign and domestic capital, upgrading economic activities and sustaining international competitiveness (beyond the well-known anti-capital government policies).

Second, employment figures cover also people employed in public works. Although it cannot be objected to bring unemployed people back into the labour market (almost totally financed by EU money), but the humiliating conditions of such activities are nearer to a „labour camp" than to a normal employment. Let alone the fact that these, mainly unskilled people cannot be integrated into a competitive labour market without education, training and retraining. Needless to say, current public work schemes do not envisage such programmes.

Third, the private sector (excepting the one-for-all car industry impact) does not offer more jobs, due to uncalculable future, lack of money and sometimes lack of reliable labour force.

Concluding remarks

For a number of reasons, as indicated in this paper, the Hungarian „economic miracle" is not sustainable. In fact, it never had been a „miracle" as reflected by macro-statistical figures and permanent government propaganda. The once-for-all factors of growth cannot be repeated or sustained. The real question is, when and in which form the unsustainability of the current economic policy will become manifest. The more the „miracle" will, at any price, be artificially sustained, the higher will be the costs and the lower the chance to find an economic development path which offers more sustainability, rebuilding competitiveness and create more social justice. Ultimately, the success does not depend any more on the implementation of a rational economic policy but on the adjustment capacity of the

Hungarian society and its readiness to change mentality and behaviour. Unfortunately, the most important victim of the „economic miracle" has been the mentally contaminated society – and it can turn out to be the main barrier to healthy, although costly, changes in the future. However, the analysis of this issue would go much beyond this economy-centered paper.

(published online mid-July 2015; Final version with small modifications: 29 October)

EU external relations

The Ukraine Crisis – Lessons for the EU

Mathias Jopp und Katrin Böttger

First lessons and recommendations for the EU's Eastern policy have to take the fact into account that in the case of Russia the EU's post-modern strategy in international relations is confronted with traditional "realpolitik" of a great (and militarily not hesitating) power.[1] It does not mean that the EU should also become a more real-political actor, a process which would anyway last decades if it were successful at all. It means considering the Russian view and world interpretation when dealing with East European affairs. It also means to invest more into studying Russia of today since after "the end of history"[2] there is too little knowledge of Russia's ambitions and of the procedures of its foreign policy-making.

Through the escalation of the crisis in Eastern Ukraine after the coming into power of a new interim government, it has also become clear that acute crisis management in the EU's neighbourhood cannot be left alone with the External Action Service and the responsible EU Commissioner. What is necessary is the involvement of important member states like Germany, France and Poland in close coordination with the other EU member states as in the case of crisis diplomacy of the three foreign ministers of the Weimar triangle in February 2014.

1. Political integration

The EU is conducting a rather ambivalent Eastern partnership. On the one hand it wants to prevent its Eastern neighbours from applying for accession to the EU. On the other hand, it tries to tie them as closely as possible to its area of integration through the transfer of norms, standards and val-

---

1 John J. Mearsheimer: "Why the Ukraine Crisis is the West's Fault, The Liberal Delusions That Provoked Putin, in: Foreign Affairs, Sept/Oct 2014, pp.1-12: http://www.foreignaffairs.com/articles/141769/john-j-mearsheimer/why-the-ukraine-crisis-is-the-wests-fault.
2 Francis Fukuyama: "The End of History?" The National Interest, Summer 1989.

ues linked to the rule of law, democracy and human rights and through the approximation of laws towards the EU acquis in the framework of the DCFTAs. The device is: Approximation to the EU through external governance yes (and as far as possible), membership no. Even if an accession perspective for Ukraine is not in the cards at present, successful transformation of Ukraine and political and economic reforms in this country are an essential interest of the EU. For such a transformation the democratic forces need be strengthened and the government and administration need to have incentives and the corresponding will for conducting the necessary reforms. This depends, on the one hand, on the fact that the rapprochement with the EU will not negatively affect the trade with Russia, which is important for a large number of oligarchs in Ukraine.[3] On the other hand, the European perspective of Ukraine needs to be made clearer. This involves various options. Beyond the recently signed association agreement Ukraine's future way could lead to a privileged partnership, an enhanced status or associate membership (without voting rights), or even membership - after the full implementation of the association agreement and total fulfilment of the necessary economic and political preconditions for accession to the EU. Whatever the incentives might be for moving from one step to the next the decisive point is to give Ukraine an orientation on its long way to Europe. Such a long-term and conditioned integration perspective for Ukraine can be used by the EU as a lever for fundamental reforms and genuine steps of Europeanization in the country. The reform menu would be long: After the holding of free and fair general elections in autumn this year, it includes a constitutional reform towards a federalisation of the state structures with representative participation of the regions, anti-corruption measures, a security sector reform and the banning of extreme right-wing political parties from government.

2. Economic integration

The conflicts about the signing of the Association Agreement including the DCFTA with Ukraine have shown that the EU needs to reconsider its free trade concept for the sake of greater flexibility and in view of a much

---

3 Piotre Kościnsúski/Ievgen Vorobiov: "Do oligarchs in Ukraine gain or lose with an EU Association Agreement?", Polish Institute of International Affairs, No. 86(539), 2013.

larger regional context implying the compatibility or even cooperation with the customs union of Russia, Belarus and Kazakhstan and the Eurasian Economic Union. Flexibility would mean facilitating trade with Russia and not hampering it. A larger economic region would build on ideas of a trade area from Lisbon to Vladivostok as suggested by the Russian president Putin and, already in 2002, by ex-Commission President Romano Prodi.[4] Envisaging such a project could lead to a win-win situation for the EU, Ukraine and Russia.

3. Relations with Russia

However, the atmosphere of EU-Russia relations has become completely poisoned in the course of the Ukraine crisis. It will take years until the lost confidence will be slowly restored. As long as there is mistrust, the EU member states need to maintain strong unity among themselves in their policy towards Russia and may seek re-assurance through NATO. But EU policy-makers must also think beyond the Ukraine crisis even if that seems to be difficult at the moment. It might become necessary to draw up some sort of a road map for the step-by-step lifting of the sanctions against Russia should the ceasefire agreement in Eastern Ukraine hold and Russia refrain from direct or indirect military engagement in the Eastern part of the country.[5] Even if that will be achievable it may well result in another frozen conflict in Eastern Europe. Such a solution cannot be in the long-term interest of the EU. In order to arrive at a lasting solution, negotiations on a bilateral level between the EU and Russia covering economic and political issues need to be re-launched at some stage in the nearer future. The objective of the EU must be to work for a stable European order by involving and not by excluding Russia.

---

4 Romano Prodi: "A wider Europe – A Proximity Policy as the Key to Stability", Brussels, 5-6 December 2002, European Commission, Press Release Database, Speech/02/619. 5) Sergey Caraganov: "How to avoid a second Afghanistan", in: Russia in Global Affairs, 6 August 2014.

4. The crisis as an opportunity for EU Eastern policy

The development in Ukraine has led to a more cohesive European foreign policy. This is true in the quantitative dimension when taking the extraordinary summits of the Heads of State and Government, the number of Foreign Ministers meetings, and the numerous contacts among the Europeans at the fringe of other events into account. And it is also true in the qualitative dimension when looking at the conclusions of the European Council, the sanctions of the EU and its member states against Russia, the mobilisation of loans of the IMF and the establishment of the Ukraine support group. The question however is whether all that signifies only acute reactions to rapidly developing events or whether a new level of integration in EU foreign policy making can be reached. Finding an answer to this question will certainly be one of the first tasks of the new personnel in Brussels. In particular the new structure of competences in the Commission with a clear hierarchy between the High Representative and the ENP Commissioner should be really implemented for improving the EU policy towards its neighbours, notably those in the East. This would mean that Mogherini would indeed exercise her right of supervision over the ENP Commissioner and, on the other hand, would take up her responsibility not only in negotiations with Iran, as Ashton did it (and as important as this may have been and will be), but also in processing the conditioned step by step policy towards the non-trustworthy Russia. In order to terminate the more or less naive attitude in foreign policy, the EU also needs to pay greater attention to the economic and security implications of its Eastern Partnership. This includes taking the power interests of Russia better into account without accommodating Russian violations of international law. In view of increasing numbers of Ukrainians killed, injured or displaced the Ukraine crisis cannot be seen as a little accident on the way towards a successful Eastern Partnership of the European Union. It requires a careful and detailed analysis of the parameters of the Neighbourhood Policy in the East in order to arrive at useful conclusions for a long-term strategy which would embrace security and stability in the same way as democracy promotion and economic development.

(published online end of October 2014)

Towards a new deal with Russia?

Susann Heinecke

The latest perception of Russia in Europe has deteroriated from being a difficult partner to being a potential enemy that not only fuels tensions in the post soviet space, but actively engages in military conflicts like as in Georgia in 2008 or in eastern Ukraine since 2014. Russia no longer hesitates to demonstrate its readiness to military confrontation and its (alleged) military power to the Europeans, among others, by ostentatiously appearing in NATO airspace with military aircraft[1]. Since the escalation of the Ukraine conflict with the annexation of Crimea by the Russian Federation in spring 2014 and the armed conflict in eastern Ukraine, EU – Russian relations seem to have reached their lowest point since the end of the Cold War. Already suffering from years of estrangement and stagnation, there appears no light at the end of the tunnel for the time being. Instead of sitting the current crisis out and waiting for the (politically) correct moment to continue business as usual, the EU should rather reconsider its policy towards Russia and move towards a more pragmatic and realistic approach.

Rhetoric and reality

In 2014, the Europeans witnessed the outbreak of another violent conflict on its continent, in eastern Ukraine. The evident involvement of Russia in fanning and maintaining this conflict has aggravated long standing tensions in EU – Russia relations that might have been predictable to the attentive observer years ago[2].

---

1 See „Russische Bomber lösen NATO-Alarm aus", Neue Zürcher Zeitung online, 29.10.2014, http://www.nzz.ch/international/europa/russische-bomber-loesen-nato-alarm-aus-1.18414344 (last access 6 May 2015).

2 The tensions have been discussed by a minority of scholars and almost not been acknowledged in the political arena.

At least since the launch of the EU's Eastern Partnership initiative in 2009, the growing potential for confrontation between Russia and the EU in Eastern Europe has become obvious. Owing to Russia claiming influence over its "near neighbourhood" regions, the six post soviet states targeted by the Eastern Partnership[3] have since then been more or less forced to make a choice between European rapprochement or closer cooperation with Russia. The launch of the Eastern Partnership itself can be interpreted as a reaction of the EU to Russia's imperialistic behaviour in Georgia in 2008, and therefore to a crisis that might be perceived as a dress rehearsal for what is happening at present. With its military engagement in Georgia in 2008, Russia could test Western patience and its willingness to support countries under pressure, and at the same time it could test its own capacities for a military engagement outside its territory. It is no surprise that the deterioration of European – Russian relations escalated in 2013 when news came of Ukraine's choice, the biggest and – from a Russian perspective – most important country in its sphere of influence[4].

However, relations had been suffering for a long time, a finding that might be surprising given the tremendous efforts of both the EU and Russia on the diplomatic stage. Since the EU enlargement dynamics reached the post soviet region (with the Baltic republics joining the EU in 2004), and in particular with regards to the military expansion of the Western sphere (NATO enlargement of 1999, 2004 and 2009)[5], Russia has felt threatened and constrained – a point of view that has constantly been ignored by the West. Rhetoric about a common space "from Lisbon to Wladiwostok" – be it from the Russian or the European side – has never really found a way into reality.

The European – respectively Western – expansion into the post soviet region coincidentally took place at a time when, on the one hand, Vladimir Putin came to power, establishing an authoritarian rule, and when Russia witnessed a remarkable and stable economic growth the first time since the establishment of market economy. Both these factors, the political sta-

---

3 Ukraine, Belarus, Moldova, Georgia, Armenia and Azerbaijan.
4 „EU leaders give Kiev until May to prove it wants to look West", Reuters, 25.2.2013, http://www.reuters.com/article/2013/02/25/us-eu-ukraine-idUSBRE91O 0U420130225 (last access 6 May 2015).
5 In 1999, Poland, Czech Republic and Hungary joined NATO, in in 2004 Bulgaria, Estonia, Latvia, Lithuania, Romania, Slovakia and Slovenia joined NATO, and in 2009 Albania and Croatia joined NATO.

bilisation and the economic recovery in the early 2000s, led to an increasing self-confidence and a self-perception of a Russia that could, after years of humiliation and domestic crisis, again constitute a great power, or at least a regional power in the post soviet territories. As a consequence, Russia did not feel adequately treated by its Western counterparts when it was considered to be an addressee of the EU's Neighbourhood policy, finding itself among countries such as Georgia, Moldova, Ukraine, the Caucasus republics and North African Mediterranean neighbouring countries. As a result, Russia was offered an alternative, higher-ranking cooperation by the EU with the concept of four common spaces that was affirmed as a new foundation for mutual cooperation in 2005. From the EU's perspective, the four common spaces concept was designed as an alternative to the Neighbourhood policy to meet Russia's special needs after its rejection of the EU's Neighbourhood approach.

In 2010, with the launch of the EU-Russia Partnership for Modernization during the EU-Russia summit in Rostov-on-Don, cooperation was upgraded again to a higher level[6]. Nevertheless, any real potential for cooperation between Russia and the EU failed to be implemented by either side due to a major misunderstanding: Whereas Russia expected a technical cooperation aiming at modernizing the country's economy and infrastructure, the EU had a broader understanding of modernization including a pluralistic society, rule of law, and respect for human and civic rights. In short, the EU had an approach of cooperation based on norms and values that were non-negotiable, whereas Russia rejected any interference into its domestic political situation. From a European point of view, any cooperation with Russia that did not take into account the norms and values the EU insisted on was considered to be dishonourable - a precondition that has, in fact, led us to where we are now.

On the wrong track

Due to these fundamentally different expectations, Russia and the EU have not suceeded in finding common ground of cooperation in recent years: Negotiations towards a renewed Partnership and Cooperation

---

6 For an overview of the EU – Russia relations, see the European External Action Service site on EU – Russia relations, http://eeas.europa.eu/russia/index_en.htm (last access 6 May 2015).

Agreement (PCA) have not advanced since their launch in 2008; the Partnership for Modernization fell into stagnation and never exceeded the level of micro-projects; and the visa dialogue has not moved forward since the Visa Facilitation Agreement of 2007. The rhetorical upgrading of relations in 2013, when the concept of "Strategic Partnership" was proclaimed[7], did not have much to do with the lack of substance that has increasingly characterized relations.

Lately, as a response to Russia's annexation of Crimea, considered by the Europeans to be illegal, and Russia's destabilizing role in Ukraine, the EU suspended negotiations for a new PCA and for a visa free regime, cancelled the 2014 EU-Russian summit, and put many projects on hold. Additionally, since March 2014, the EU has imposed sanctions on Russia in the form of asset freezing, visa bans and economic sanctions[8]. Last but not least, the Europeans agreed with its Western partners to temporarily exclude Russia from the Group of Eight (G8), returning to the G7 format without Russia, and deprived Russia from its G8 presidency that it held in 2014. As a response, Russia has taken measures including a ban on certain food imports from European countries. Symbolically, Russia's head of state president Putin is conspicuous by his absence from high-level international meetings, for instance from the Davos World Economic Forum in January 2015. To summarise, Russia's distance from Europe has widened enormously and mutual confidence has been deeply shattered.

Driven by events, the EU in 2014 has turned from an approach with moderate conditions to a rigorous isolationist approach, aiming at bringing Russia to reason by cutting its economic and political room for manoeuvre. Unfortunately, to date, this isolationist approach has not solved any of the outlined problems and has aggravated some of the existing challenges of the EU – Russia relationship:

• It pushes Russia further away from Europe and the West, compels the country to enforce its own regional integration projects (Eurasian Union), and leads to a further isolation of Russia instead of its integration into the international community;

---

7 For the strategic partnership idea, see http://eeas.europa.eu/top_stories/2013/030613 _eu-russia_en.htm (last access 6 May 2015).
8 For details, see http://europa.eu/newsroom/highlights/special-coverage/eu_sanction s/index_en.htm (last access 7 May 2015).

- It encourages Russia to continue and enhance its "divide et impera" approach towards single EU member states, aimed at benefitting from advantageous bilateral cooperation and weakening the EU as a whole;
- It reduces any opportunities to calm the situation and rebuild confidence;
- It does not solve the conflict in Ukraine, or any other frozen conflict in the post soviet region;
- It not only fails to further the democratization or modernization of Russia, but carries the risk of destabilizing Russia and enforcing president Putins authoritarian rule;
    - It does not take into account the situation in Russia and president Putin's motivation for his tough authoritarian and neo-imperialistic rule – the maintenance of his own power.
    - To put it simply: The EU's past approach towards Russia has led to nowhere. The EU should take the opportunity to find a more realistic and pragmatic approach towards relations that takes account of Russian interests and the conditions arising from the political reality in Russia.

Beyond illusions: towards a pragmatic approach

Which options do we then have? First, the EU could continue or even enforce the isolationist approach including sanctions, the temporary freezing of cooperation projects and the occasional exclusion of Russia from the international community. In the medium term, the EU could continue to reduce its energy dependence on Russia via a common energy strategy, including all EU member states, and thus try to cut ties with Russia as much as possible. However, it is very improbable that all EU member states with their very different interests and attitudes towards Russia would agree to one consistent policy. Moreover, this approach has unpredictable consequences with regards to Russia's future and leaves Europe uncertain about its biggest Eastern neighbour.

Secondly, the EU could gradually return to the customized and broad cooperation agenda, ignoring the reasons that once led to the suspension of that cooperation - the annexation of Crimea and the Russian destabilizing interference in Ukraine. In that case, the EU would lose its credibility and, most probably, restore the problems and inadequacies of its policy towards Russia. Relations would suffer under the same misunderstandings and ineffectiveness as it did even before the Ukraine crisis. Furthermore, many questions would remain unanswered: How to proceed with the Modernization Partnership, as long as the notion of "modernization" is not clear to both partners? How can a European security order be drawn up as long as there is distrust and hostility? How can Eurasian integration and European integration be linked to each other, for example in its economic dimension? Would it be possible to integrate some countries in both the Eurasian Union and the EU, and how?

These questions certainly have to be faced and answered in the long run. Meanwhile, a third alternative could help both the EU and Russia out of the crisis: a pragmatic approach led by the desire for cooperation in areas where common interests exist. This would certainly cover the established trade and investment relations, bringing together markets and business people and increasing the economic interconnection of Russia in the world. For that purpose, the current sanctions and contraints should be lifted, especially as their effect is controversial. Furthermore, to facilitate people-to-people contacts, the EU should, in the end, establish a visa-free regime for Russian citizens. By increasing the contacts and exchanges between people, the EU could demonstrate its liberal values and serve as an attractive example. With regards to the current conflict in Ukraine, an international peacekeeping initiative under UN mandate could help depoliticize the situation and free both the EU and Russia from the impasse.

The EU member states have to get together seriously and discuss their common – and single bilateral – interests towards Russia, without hiding themselves behind nice-sounding declarations. Finally, in the long term, the EU cannot avoid starting a dialogue with Russia on their future relationship from an economic and political perspective and in terms of security. Crucial issues that have to be covered are the regional cooperation of the EU and Eurasian Union, the role and borders of NATO and Russia's relations with the alliance, the role of Russia as a regional power, the EU's relations with its Eastern neighbours, and much more. Even if these questions have been on the agenda for years, they have obviously not been properly and consistently addressed. Interestingly enough, Russian foreign minister Sergey Lavrov raised the same question that was already posed 20 years ago, a question that brings it to the point and that is still awaiting a satisfying answer: Do we want a European order *with Russia, without*

Russia, or against Russia?[9] It might be difficult and unpleasant – but Europe can't escape that question.

(published online mid-Mai 2015)

---

9 Sergey Lavrov asked the question in the context of the security architecture, see speech of Russian foreign minister Sergey Lavrov at the 51st Munich Security Conference on 7 February 2015, http://www.russland.ru/lawrow-auf-der-muenchner-sic herheitskonferenz/ (last access 7 May 2015). The notion dates from the mid-1990s and had constantly been used, among others, by German foreign minister Klaus Kinkel (1992-1998) or federal chancellor Gerhard Schröder (1998-2005).

Highway to hell? - European Union's Eastern Policy from a Civilian power perspective

Michael Meimeth, Jarosław Jańczak

There is no doubt that the enlargement of the EU to now include 28 member states can be seen as the most successful exercise in preventive diplomacy and projection of political stability, democratic peace and economic prosperity since the Roman Empire. The downside of this success story of European Union enlargement, however, is that it has complicated the relationship between the EU and Russia and has led, step-by-step, to a political destabilization on the eastern boundaries of the EU. In this respect, the Eastern Partnership initiative, launched by the European Union in 2008 to cover the eastern dimension of its already existing European Neighborhood Policy was a major turning point. Prior to the Eastern Partnership Summit in Vilnius in late November 2013, Russia exerted intense pressure on its neighborhood states not to accept the EU's initiative and it was successful in the case of Ukraine. At the Vilnius summit, Ukrainian President Yanukovich refused to sign an Association Agreement with the EU. His decision not to sign the Agreement led to violent public protests in Kiev which culminated in President Yanukovich's overthrow on February 22, 2014. As a result, Russia invaded and annexed the Crimean peninsula and actively supported pro-Russian separatist forces fighting the Ukrainian army in a bloody and violent conflict in the eastern part of Ukraine (Larsen 2014).

All these events, taking most Western government officials by surprise, represent a major geopolitical shock to the Post Cold War European Security order. While slowing down the European Union's initiatives on Eastern Partnership for the time being, the crisis over Ukraine also calls for an urgent reassessment of the underlying political discourses on Europe as an international actor shaping the European Union's attempts to promote the political and economic integration and/or association of its eastern neighbours: particularly influential in this context has been conception of the EU as a "civilian" or "normative" power.

Michael Meimeth, Jarosław Jańczak

The EU as a "civilian power" in international politics

There is a widespread consensus in the European political as well as academic discourse that the European Union plays a distinctive role in international politics (Hyde-Price 2008). The idea that the EU is a distinctive, qualitatively new and better international actor was first outlined by François Duchêne in the early 1970's when he referred to the EU as an "example of a new stage in political civilization. The European Community in particular would have a chance to demonstrate the [international, M.M.] influence which can be wielded by a large political cooperative formed to exert essentially civilian forms of power" (Duchêne 1973, 19). This is often (critically) compared to the USA's (international) policy based on classical tools, including the usage of military power. Since the European Community is a "civilian group of countries with a long history of economic power and relatively short on armed force" (ibd., 20), it has a fundamental interest in trying to domesticate relations between states. From the perspective of the domestication of international relations, "civilian powers" like the EU essentially pursue the following aims (Harnisch/- Maull 2001, 4):

- Constraining the use of force through cooperation and collective security arrangements;
- Strengthening the rule of law through multilateral cooperation, integration and partial transfer of sovereignty;
- Promoting democracy and human rights within and between states.

It is quite obvious that this list of "civilian aims" reflects to a very large extent the political structure and values upon which the European Union is built on. Because of its unique and innovative internal political and institutional structure, the EU has no other choice but to project these principles and norms in its external relations. For the EU, acting as a "force for good" in international relations is the compelling consequence of the internal logic of the European integration process (Orbie 2006, 125-126). Not surprisingly, the academic discourse on EU as a "civilian" power has been favourably received by the European political establishment. Central elements of the "civilian power" concept can be found in various official EU documents and speeches of EU officials. The most comprehensive and most clear document on the European Union's identity as an international actor however is the European Security Strategy of 2003 entitled "A secure Europe in a better world" which is a "well-written description of the EU's role concept as civilian force" in world politics (Maull 2005, 792).

It is in the context of this European political and academic discourse on the EU's international identity that the enlargement process as well as the Eastern Partnership Initiative gain its specific meaning. From the perspective of the "civilian power" discourse, both the enlargement process as well as the Partnership Initiative were and still are all about transferring and diffusing the EU's internal values and norms to the states of Central and Eastern Europe allowing a post-national order to replace the logic of power politics that governed this part of Europe until the end of the Cold War. The transformative power of the EU was based for the most part, if not exclusively on its own distinctive polity and its influence on the Central and Eastern European states, stemming not from what the EU does, but what it is (Manners 2008).

However a "civilian" or "normative power" driven enlargement process of the EU has serious downsides. First of all, from this perspective the enlargement of the EU cannot be anything other than open-ended, lending the project - in fact – a universal nature. Since the purpose of civilizing international relations exclusively based on the norms and principles outlined above has a global and/or universal dimension, the geographical limitation of EU enlargement is to a large extent excluded. Moreover, the open-ended nature of the enlargement process is one of the key factors in preserving the EU's legitimacy to promote its norms and values beyond its boundaries. As has been pointed out by a Finnish analyst, the EU's attempts to divorce its normative power from the accession process run the risk of being counterproductive. Therefore, the Eastern Partnership Initiative represents both the avoidance and the continuation of enlargement by other means (Haukkala 2008), being an instrument designed both to let the partner states in and to keep them out. To summarize, both the EU's enlargement policy and its Partnership Initiative seem to end up as a form of "soft imperialism" since each enlargement round creates new boundaries beyond which the European Norms and values have to be imposed if the EU wants to counter the concerns over the "fortress Europe" idea (Haukkala 2008).

It is obvious that this "imperial logic" inherent in the "civilian power" concept has a strong potential for conflict when third powers perceive EU's strategies on its eastern boundaries as a zero-sum game and are determined enough to loudly articulate this perception as well as strong enough to undertake counteractions. And this is exactly what happened in the case of Ukraine when Russia very quickly developed a hostile zero-sum attitude to the EU's growing influence in this region as a result of the Eastern Partnership initiative. This hostile zero-sum attitude has been furhter intensified by the fact that major member states like Germany have shown, at least up to now, little understanding for Russia's interests in containing the EU because they perceive the latter as an inherently benign civilian power (Larsen 2014, 17). Since the "civilian power" concept rests on the assumption that there are cosmopolitan norms and values which transcend the particular or even rival claims of states or other political entities, the eastward expansion of the EU might never be seen by the EU as a threat to Russia. On the contrary, any opposition to further initiatives to promote the "European project" further eastward might be perceived as a threat to the EU's vision of establishing a post-national order in Europe based on democratic values, international harmony and effective multilateralism. From this perspective there is no other way for the European Union other than to "punish" recalcitrant opponents like Russia. "Punishing" Russia by imposing ever increasing sanctions, as carried out by the EU in the recent past, is an extremely dangerous and conflict prone strategy because it makes an already bad situation even worse (Mearsheimer 2014).

With this perspective in mind, the fundamental problem with the EU's foreign policy in general and its eastern policy in particular becomes very clear: the European Union still clings to a "civilian" model of international relations which relies on the promotion of norms and values and explicitly eschews traditional power politics while at the same time the boundaries of the EU seem to require a much different role model that bears directly on the anarchic structure of the international system. A brief excursus on geopolitics and geopolitical models of the European Union might further develop this assessment of the civilian power concept as being largely inappropriate for the EU to cope with the challenges emanating from international politics.

Geopolitics and geopolitical models of the European Union – changing paradigms and perceptions

The concept of the EU as a "civilian power" has been implemented under the very specific political-territorial conditions of post-Cold War Europe. They were characterized by an absence of strong competing centers of integration in the neighborhood after the collapse of the Soviet Union. Consequently the expansion of the EU was based on structuring its internal and external borders according to one of four strategies: *networked (non)border, march, colonial frontier* and *limes* (Browning and Joenniemi 2008). In the case of a networked (non)border, state boundaries were gradually eroding together with free flows of people and goods, which was coordinated by numerous local centers. A *march* corresponds with a buffer zone (Browning and Joenniemi, 2008, p. 527; Walters, 2004), a *colonial frontier* is a line, constantly pushed forward and separating asymmetric structures. The line itself is one dimensionally permeable, with norms and values being transferred from a more developed partner to the less advanced one. A *limes* represents a final border, however also separating asymmetric structures (Browning and Joenniemi, 2008, p. 529; Walters, 2004). In the practice of EUrope structuring its borders, it seems that the *networked (non)border* has been applied in the case of western European non-member states, limes for Mediterranean neighbors. The continental east was seen as *colonial frontier*, that was to replace *march*.

However the considerations outlined above reveal even more – they give a more general picture of the geopolitical model of the EU. Christopher Browning and Pertti Joenniemi (2008) identify three of them: Westphalian, imperial and neomedieval. The first one has a clearly determined space, enclosed within precisely designed state(-like) boundaries. The center controls the entire territory on a basis of the equal exercising of norms, values and laws. In the case of the European Union one can see it as a semi-state structure (Caporaso, 1996), with defined territory marked and protected by the external boundary (Schengen boundary), *acquis communautaire* being here the legal base for the whole territory and the new political center taking over powers and responsibilities from the member states (Browning and Joenniemi, 2008, pp. 522-526). The second assumes that the center and peripheries can be identified, with the former producing ideas and solutions transferred to the latter. The further from the center, the weaker the influence is. The center is consequently surrounded by circles of a concentric character. Both the enlargements and external involvement illustrate this model in the case of the EU (Zielonka, 2007), with the European Neighborhood Policy as an example (Browning and Joenniemi, 2008, pp. 522-526). The neomedieval model assumes there is no single dominating center, and several regional and local functionally networked centers can be identified (Wind, 2003).

The territorially and normatively expansive character of the EU allows us to classify it as the imperial model (Zielonka, 2007). Consequently the logic of concentric circles can be applied, where the very core is made up of the most integrated (institutionally and non-institutionally) group of member states. The further away from the core, the less intensive the participation in the integration project (Comelli, Greco, Tocci, 2007). Outer circles consequently reveal those areas not participating in the euro zone, the Schengen zone, further away the non-member candidates, then potential candidates, and finally the partner states.

The dynamics illustrated here have at least three significant consequences for understanding the Eastern policies of the EU. First of all, it is the expanding character of the EU *project*, following the neo-functional linearity (Lindberg, 1963) of territorial and functional spill over. It is attracting (and is trying to attract) more and more states located further and further from the original center. Consequently the EU has been growing in size. But the newly 'absorbed' territories' link to the center diminishes the further they are away from the center. Secondly, the borders of the *European project* are much wider than the borders of the EU, representing in addition more of a frontier scheme than a boundary one. They are often fuzzy and undefined, with constantly changing locations, further and further away. The geostrategy of a *colonial frontier* describes its character in the eastern part of the continent, with neighboring states as an expansion space. Here the EU, as the normative power, exports norms and values, stabilizing, democratizing and developing the outer circles. Thirdly, both academic reflection and the political practice of the *European project* have been strongly Europe-centric. For over two decades they have assumed (directly or indirectly) that the EU is a dominating (or even a single existing) project in this part of the world, representing a kind of civilized space surrounded by 'barbarian' territories. This perception resulted from economic (high GDP) and political (liberal democracy) asymmetries, but also from a lack of alternative 'gravity centers' located in the neighborhood. Consequently, the *European project* was treated and developed as if surrounded by 'no man's land,' expanding almost without limit towards the outer spaces.

However this Europe-centric perspective was undermined by the "recovery" of Russia and her attempt to reconstruct her own empire in the 2010s. Consequently the conflict in Ukraine can be seen as an outcome of the overlapping influences of two competing centers: Brussels and Moscow. Both are exporting their projects to the neighboring territories, creating outer circles. Ukraine is consequently a frontier for both sides, a space where the political, economic and cultural influences of Brussels and Moscow are penetrating and overlap. This situation has been acceptable for both sides until recently, motivated however by various factors: The EU, tired with the 2004/7/13 big bang, was not able to offer very close relations, for example membership, to its eastern neighbors. At the same time Russia had (almost) no means or resources to prevent Ukraine from implementing its western orientation. The treatment of Ukraine as a form of colonial frontier meant that in practice it became a sort of march, geopolitically separating both parties.

But the 2013 Eastern Partnership Vilnius Summit created a situation where both projects suddenly became mutually exclusive. The signing of the association agreement would mean further expansion of the EU, colliding with the Russian offer of the Eurasian Economic Union. The previous forms of influence tolerated *frontier* borders (or even *march*), the new one was based on an either-or principle. This had to lead to the (re)boundarization of the border between the *European project* and the *Russian project*. The question has been where it is to be located (the cause of the territorial disputes) and how is it going to be settled (confronting the EU's normative power with the Russian form of intervention which follows a traditional means of power)?

The line of argument presented above makes it necessary to redefine the nature of both projects. The exclusivity and the potential for conflict corresponds much better with the Westphalian model (Caporaso, 1996), also with regard to the instruments of external policies. Both structures cannot go on expanding indefinitely, blocking each other territorially, but also politically, economically, and – in the case of Russia - militarily. The overlapping of influences is no longer an option, a boundary between both structures has to be established. Consequently Ukraine can belong either to the *European project*, or the *Russian project*. This can include its entire territory or can alternatively lead to its disintegration. In any case one can expect the geostrategy of *limes* being applied by both sides, with the new boundary being "final" for them. This opens – together with the previously debated criticism of the civilian power concept – a window of opportunity for a neo-realist perspective.

The (neo-)realist perspective – an alternative?

The basic tenet of the neo-realist or structural realist perspective on is that the pressures stemming from the international system "shape" and "shove" the behavior of states without completely determining this behavior. The structure of the international system is – in principle – anarchic. Anarchy here is by no means chaos – it simply means that states as sovereign entities are formally equal with each other and are not subordinated to a higher authority which has a system wide law making and law enforcing authority. Therefore, international politics have no authority bound by law and there is no international police force to rely on. It is rather a realm in which states have to figure out by themselves how they want to live with each other, how they are to manage their relationship and ultimately how they are going to manage their security concerns as well as their own survival as a sovereign entity. So far, international politics can be described as a realm of self-help or as a self-help system. Given the anarchic structure of the international system, some degree of security competition especially between the great powers is persistent and – more important – inevitable. Balancing and the strong tendency of shaping the international environment conducive to their own strategic interests and preferences has become the dominant feature of great power behaviour (Waltz 1979, 78-128).

From this perspective, the European Union' s role in international politics cannot be seen primarily as an exporter of norms and values, but as a collective actor whose primary concern is to secure its survival under the conditions of international anarchy. To this end, the European Union serves three main purposes for its member states:

1. It serves as an instrument to preserve and promote the international economic competiveness of its member states in the light of the challenges of globalization.
2. It serves as instrument for the EU member states to meet the geopolitical challenges.
3. It serves as an instrument for collectively shaping the European Union's regional international environment according to its own political, economic and security interests (Hyde-Price 2006, 222).

The latter purpose become increasingly prominent in the early 1990s when the European Union's well-being was threatened by the prospect of political instability and economic crisis within the post-communist Central and

Eastern European states. And it is these international pressures which have led the EU to gradually shape its regional international environment, establishing a blend of imposed and negotiated order in its neighboring territories. Far from being a "civilian" or "normative power", the European Union's transformative power in Central and Eastern Europe was based on its economic clout, the fear of exclusion from its attractive economic market and the promise of future membership (Hyde-Price 2008, 31). Therefore, by projecting stability into its eastern regional environment in this specific way, the European Union acquired the classical role of an ordering power on the European continent (Hyde-Price 2006, 226).

If the EU acknowledges its role as that of a European ordering power rather than clinging to the self-image of being an exporter of values and norms in international politics, it would not only mean that the agenda outlined above of a "civilian power" would be seriously constrained by the structural pressures of the self-help system. It would also allow it to design the eastern enlargement process of the European Union as a clearly defined geographical project whose boundaries would largely depend for a large part upon the degree of security competition between the EU and Russia. Both the European Union and Russia have – as Hedley Bull has already pointed out in his seminal analysis of the role of great powers in an anarchical society – a special obligation to dampen their security competition in order to preserve and promote a stable and peaceful international order (Bull 1977, pp 200). Accepting a role model inspired by neo-realist logic would allow the EU to tone down its "civilian power" discourse while at the same time being better primed to resolve great power conflicts on the basis of reciprocity!

Conclusion

It has been argued in this paper that the "civilian" or "normative power" model which is shaping the EU's efforts towards the political and economic integration or association of its eastern neighbours is not only for the most part inefficient but is also prone to conflict when it comes to the management of boundary problems related with this process. A brief excursus on the geopolitical models of the European Union supports this assessment. In contrast to the "civilian power" model, by recognizing that there are enduring security competition and rival interests between states given the anarchic structure of the international system, the neorealist perspective opens up space for compromise and – at least – a partial resolution of conflicts. However, even if there is some virtue in the neorealist argument in this context, there is a strong indication that the challenges of managing the boundary problems related to the European Union's eastern policy will become increasingly detrimental to the core values on which the European Union is based on – democracy, the rule of law, transforming the notion of sovereignty, eschewing and rejecting traditional power politics. If the European Union is not be able to reconcile in its foreign policy the competing logic of being a "civilian power" (which is of crucial importance for the success of the European integration process itself) with the logic of international anarchy, it runs the risk of ending up as a tragic international actor finding itself on a highway to hell. To find a viable exit from this highway will constitute an immediate challenge for the European Union's credibility and legitimacy as a serious international actor!

References:

Browning, Christopher S., Pertti Joenniemi (2008), Geostrategies of the European Neighbourhood Policy, "European Journal of International Relations", Vol. 14, No. 3.

Bull, Hedley (1977), The Anarchical Society, New York 1977 Caporaso, James A. (1996), The European Union and Forms of State: Westphalian, Regulatory or Post-Modern?, "Journal of Common Market Studies", Vol. 34.

Comelli, Michele, Ettore Greco, Nathalie Tocci (2007), From Boundary to Borderland: Transforming the Meaning of Borders through the European Neighbourhood Policy, "European Foreign Affairs Review", No. 12.

Duchêne, François (1973), The European Community and the the Uncertainties of Interdependence, in: Kohnstamm/Hager (eds) A Nation Writ Large, London 1973.

Harnisch, Sebastian/Maull, Hanns W. (2001), Introduction, in: Harnsich/Maull (eds), Germany as a Civilian Power?, Manchester 2001.

Haukkala, Hiski (2008), The European Union as a Regional Normative Hegemon, Europe-Asia Studies 9/2008.

Hyde-Price, Adrian (2006), Normative Power Europe: A Realist Critique, Journal of European Public Policy 2/2006.

Hyde-Price, Adrian (2008), A"Tragique Actor"? A Realist Perspective on "Ethical Power Europe", International Affairs 84/2008.

Larsen, Henrik Boesen (2014), Great Power Politics and the Ukraine Crisis: NATO, EU and Russia after 2014, Report 18/2014, Copenhagen DIIS.

Lindberg, Leon N. (1963), The Political Dynamics of European Economic Integration, Stanford University Press, Stanford, CA. Manners, Ian (2002), Normative power Europe: A Contradiction in Terms?. Journal of Common Market Studies, 2/2002.

Maull, Hanns W. (2005), Europe and the New Balance of Global Order, International Affairs 81/2005.

Mearsheimer, John (2014), Conference Call with John Mearsheimer on the Ukraine Crisis, September 4, 2014, https:/www.foreignaffairs.com/press/conference-call-me arsheimer-john-ukraine-crisis

Orbie, Jan (2006), Civilian Power Europe: Review of the Original and Current Debates, Cooperation and Conflict 41/2006.

Walters, Wiliam (2004), The Frontiers of the European Union: A Geostrategic Perspective, "Geopolitics", Vol. 9, No. 3.

Waltz, Kenneth N. (1979), Theory of International Politics, Reading, Mass. 1979.

Wind, Marlene (2003), The European Union as a polycentric polity: returning to a neo-medieval Europe?, [in:] European Constitutionalism beyond the State, J.H.H. Weiler, M. Wind (eds.), Cambridge University Press, Cambridge.

Zielonka, Jan (2007), Europe as Empire. The Nature of the Enlarged European Union, Oxford University Press, Oxford.

(published online end of Mai 2015)

Transatlantic Relations under Obama's Presidency: Between Dream and Reality

Anna Dimitrova

US-EU Relations: Time for Assessment

On 4 November 2014, Democrats and President Obama had not just another bad night. The mid-term elections held on that day brought a huge success to the Republicans who succeeded not only in keeping a comfortable majority in the House of Representatives, but also in taking away majority from Democrats in the Senate. The power shift on Capitol Hill will certainly have international consequences. Most importantly, it could have an impact on the transatlantic relationship, since the Republicans are expected to put pressure on President Obama to take more decisive actions in terms of foreign policy, in particular regarding the enforcement of firmer sanctions against Russia's involvement in the Ukrainian crisis and Iran's nuclear program.

Meanwhile, on the other side of the Atlantic, some important changes took place, too. The representatives of the three main EU institutions handed down the mandate to their successors. On 1 November 2014, the former President of the Eurogroup Jean-Claude Juncker succeeded Jose Manuel Barroso as President of the European Commission, while Italy's former Minister of Foreign Affairs Federica Mogherini replaced Catherine Ashton as Vice President of the European Commission and High Representative of the Union for Foreign Affairs and Security Policy. Last, but not least, on 1 December 2014, the Belgian Herman Van Rompuy, the first President of the European Council since the introduction of that position by the Lisbon Treaty in 2009 was replaced by the former Prime Minister of Poland Donald Tusk. Three new faces for Europe that President Obama needs to get familiar to and work with during his last two years in office – not an easy task for him knowing that, as he himself expressed it, he had some difficulties remembering "who is who" in Europe and getting used to the fact that when dialling "Europe's phone number" he can be put through to three different persons. Before looking in the future, it seems to be the right moment for assessing the state of transatlantic relations under Obama's Presidency so far.

Barack Obama's victory in the 2008 US presidential elections did not bring about a new golden age in transatlantic relations, as many Europeans initially expected. Of course, compared to the Bush' years of unilateralist and hard power-driven foreign policy disrespecting European allies unless they agree to align with US interests and take part in a "coalition of the willing", tone and style of US-European relations changed significantly as the new Administration tried hard to renew American leadership on "moral and exemplary" basis[1], as well as to put the US foreign policy back on a multilateral and "multi-partner[2]" track by pursuing what can be regarded as a "smart diplomacy"[3] strategy. However, as a matter of substance, there has been no significant change in transatlantic relations. Shortly after stepping into office, President Obama openly declared that America's security priorities had shifted from the Old continent towards economically and militarily rising Asia, and even identified himself as "America's first Pacific President"[4].

Actually, during Obama's presidency there has been neither a drift nor a radical change in transatlantic relations, but rather they have been marked by ups and downs. Five main phases in the evolution of the US-European relations could thus be identified.

---

1 Barack Obama, "Renewing American Leadership", Foreign Affairs, July/August 2007.
2 Council on Foreign Relations Address by Secretary of State Hillary Clinton, CFR, July 15, 2009.
3 The concept of « smart power » was first introduced by Suzanne Nossel ("Smart Power", Foreign Affairs, March/April, 2004) to stress the importance of finding the right balance between military (hard power) and diplomatic (soft power) tools in foreign policy. In her Confirmation Hearing as nominee for Secretary of State in 2009, Hillary Clinton officially adopted the concept of "smart power" by defining it as "the full range of tools at our disposal – diplomatic, economic, military, political, legal, and cultural – picking the right tool or combination of tools for each situation" and stated that "the smart power diplomacy will be the vanguard of our foreign policy" (Transcript of Hilary Clinton's Confirmation Hearing, January 13, 2009).
4 Remarks by President Barack Obama at Suntory Hall, November 14, 2009.

Phase One: the Honeymoon

The first phase in transatlantic relations started even before Obama stepped in the White House. It was a very short but at the same time a very intensive and rich in emotions phase opened up by then candidate for presidency Obama's 2008 Berlin speech in which he forcefully declared that "America has no better partner than Europe" and that it "needs a strong European Union that deepens the security and prosperity of this continent, while extending a hand abroad"[5] . Only one speech was enough for candidate Obama to conquer Europeans' hearts and minds, eager for change after Bush' "go-it-alone" era. Public opinion polls spoke about Europe's "Obamamania"[6] and "Obamaeuphoria" given the very high level of support which Europeans granted to Obama - 69% of Europeans viewed Senator Obama favorably in 2008 with the highest ratings being in France (85%), the Netherlands (85%) and Germany (83%) against only 19% of approval for Bush[7]. Despite the fact that Obama barely mentioned Europe during his first presidential campaign, his popularity in the Old continent stood almost unaffected.

Nevertheless, the US-EU honeymoon phase, as pictured by the Europeans, lasted as long as the honeymoon "lol". The first event that put an end to the European dream-like condition came from the decision made by President Obama to skip the 24-25 May US-EU Madrid summit in 2010 as a result of "excessive summitry"[8]. After having visited Europe six times in 2009 and attended US-EU summits in Prague and Washington, Obama made it clear that he was "fairly unimpressed" with the transatlantic summits and therefore unwilling to go to any further meetings that "risk lacking substance"[9]. The second blow that entirely cooled Europeans' enthusiasm off was Obama's no-show at the 20th Berlin Wall Anniversary celebration on November 9, 2009 drawing heated criticism on both sides of the Atlantic as expressed by Rich Lowry, editor of National Review, who contended that "Obama's failure to go to Berlin is the most telling non-

---

5 Barack Obama, "2008 Speech in Berlin".
6 "Obamamania Abroad", Pew Research Global Attitudes Project, July 16, 2008.
7 Transatlantic Trends 2008, The German Marshall Fund.
8 "Obama's Madrid snub exposes 'excessive' EU summitry", EurActiv, February 2, 2010.
9 "Barack Obama is to skip a US-EU summit due in May", BBC, February 2, 2010.

event of his presidency. It's hard to imagine any other American president eschewing the occasion"[10].

During this phase, some US-EU friction also appeared concerning the war in Afghanistan. The latter became the apple of discord in late 2009 after President Obama announced a surge of 30,000 US troops to Afghanistan while at the same time setting up the end of 2014 as a deadline for withdrawal. In reaction to that, some EU countries, including France, took a very critical stance towards this strategy and started rushing to retreat their troops from the field, thus putting at risk, according to Obama, the successful accomplishment of the operation.

Phase Two: Back to Reality

What put a further strain on the US-European relations was the economic reality itself. The ever-growing amount of US public debt that exceeded 100% of GDP for the first time in 2011 drove the adoption of the Budget Control Act (BCA) by Congress that imposed the so-called "sequestration process", i. e. automatic spending cuts, especially with regard to the defense budget. In order to meet strict budget constraints and avoid a fiscal cliff, the Pentagon put forward a new doctrine of "burden sharing" and "smart defense" that requires from the European allies to take fully their part of responsibility and cost. But, the economic crisis also hit the other side of the Atlantic where public debt skyrocketed, especially in the Southern EU countries, thus making European governments commit themselves to implement austerity measures and limit spending in all spheres, including security and defense.

This phase was particularly marked by the farewell speech of former US Secretary of Defense Robert Gates. Before leaving office in July 2011, Gates spoke on the future of transatlantic relations by bluntly stating that NATO had turned into a "two-tiered alliance" divided between the "soft" and the "hard" member states. While the "soft" ones, in his view, specialize in "humanitarian, development, peacekeeping, and talking tasks", the "hard" ones conduct military operations. The "hard" members thus invest a lot in the alliance and bear almost the whole burden, whereas the "soft"

---

10 Rich Lawry, "Behind Obama's Berlin Wall Snub", Real Clear Politics, November 3, 2009.

members, according to Gates, only take profit from their membership without really engaging in the alliance and take their true responsibility. To support his words with facts, Gates pointed out that "just five of 28 allies – the US, the UK, France, Germany, along with Albania – exceed the agreed 2% of GDP spending on defense". In 2014, the situation looks even worse because, according to NATO data, only three EU member states (France and Germany are no longer part of this group) meet the 2% target, namely Britain, Greece and Estonia. It is therefore obvious that the long lasting US calling on EU member states and especially on those who are also NATO members, to increase defense spending so as to face new threats is like a voice in the desert.

The NATO capability gap issue was in particular put forward during the 2011 intervention in Libya. Despite the fact that several EU countries officially took part in the UN-led international coalition, only two of them, namely France and the UK, provided military forces to enforce a no-fly zone so as to protect civilians from Kaddafi's armed forces. In reality, the Libyan crisis generated both intra-European and transatlantic tensions. On the one hand, while France and the UK, both permanent members at the UN Security Council, cast an affirmative vote for Resolution 1973 (2011) authorizing "all necessary measures" to protect civilians and establish a "no-fly zone" over Libya, Germany, a holder of a non-permanent member seat at that moment, abstained from voting, thus clearly expressing its reserves regarding a military intervention against Kaddafi's regime. On the other hand, although the French and the British took the lead of the operation, it soon turned out that their military capability was quite limited, a fact that made the US abandon its "leading from behind"[11] tactic and give a solid hand to its European partners by letting NATO enter the game and take command over the no-fly zone over Libya.

Although NATO's operation in Libya was hailed as "a model intervention" that reaffirmed that the "alliance remains an essential source of stability"[12] for its rapid response to the deteriorating situation in the country, it also made it obvious that Europe could still not be considered as a full security partner for out of the three leading EU military forces, Germany opted out of the intervention, while France and the UK clearly showed they lacked equipment to carry out correct targeting and airstrikes. As a

---

11 Ryan Lizza, "Leading from Behind", The New Yorker, April 26, 2011.
12 Ivo Daalder and James Stavridis, "NATO's Victory in Libya", Foreign Affairs, March/April 2012.

result of that, there was no real burden sharing between the US and its European allies given the fact that the US provided 75% of the intelligence, surveillance, reconnaissance data, and military equipment in the operation[13].

Phase Three: the US Pivot to Asia

Phase two undoubtedly paved the way for phase three. It was almost no surprise when the Pentagon revealed in its January 2012 "Strategic Guidance" that America's new defense strategy will from now on be a balance shift to Asia-Pacific. What became famously known as the "US pivot to Asia" actually aims at rebalancing the US military presence and investment in Europe where the majority of countries are considered by the Pentagon as "producers of security rather than consumers of it", towards the Asia-Pacific region where containing China's military rise and potential threat has now become a strategic priority for Washington.

Against this background, the "US pivot to Asia" is generally seen as a "natural, if long overdue"[14] reaction to Europe's inability to act as a security provider without counting on the US security umbrella. Moreover, at time of pressures for spending cuts imposed on Washington by the 2011 BCA, American officials see Europe as the best arena to disengage. Not only does the Old continent no longer represent any major threat for the US interests and the international security but also, as the Financial Times chief foreign affairs commentator Gideon Rachman outlined, "it has made the US lose its patience because of Europe's inability to act on its own"[15]. In addition to that, the "US pivot to Asia" can also be seen as a strategy of Realpolitik adopted by the Obama's Administration to face the new balance of power triggered by the "global power shift", i.e. "the transfer of power from West to East" that occurred at the beginning of 2000s and is driven by the rapid economic growth of some emerging markets, famously

---

13 Idem.
14 Jonathan Masters, "The Pentagon Pivots to Asia", Council on Foreign Relations Analysis Brief, January 6, 2012.
15 Gideon Rachman, "The Pivot: Test of Europe as a Security Actor?", GMF Policy Brief, Transatlantic SecurityTask Force Series, May 2013, p. 2.

known as the "BRIC"[16]. Consequently, the debate of a transatlantic drift took front stage during this phase. Some analysts like Michael Cox even argued that "in a world where economic power is shifting eastwards towards Asia, the transatlantic relationship is bound (at worst) to become irrelevant, or likely (at best) to become far less important"[17], while others pointed out that "the relatively limited US involvement in Libya may be a sign of things to come, as America becomes less willing to carry the greater burden in interventions in Europe's neighborhood"[18]. However, what seems problematic about the US retrenchment from Europe is to know if it will really make European countries spend more on defense, or if it will rather make them more inward-looking and unwilling to engage abroad.

Phase Four: the PRISM Scandal

The scandal that broke out in June 2013 following former NSA (National Security Agency) contractor Edward Snowden's revelations regarding the existence of a top-secret surveillance program code-named PRISM[19] aimed at processing electronic personal data including that of EU citizens and officials, strained further transatlantic relations. Some pundits even hurried to declare that "the public outrage that the affair has spawned could potentially be more damaging to the transatlantic relationship than the Iraq war was a decade ago"[20]. Although the disclosure of PRISM mass surveillance activities provoked an outrage across Europe, there was no coherent EU reaction and messages sent to Washington by the EU institu-

---

16 The acronym depicting Brazil, Russia, India and China was first introduced by the economist Jim O'Neill in his paper "Building Better Global Economic BRICs", Goldman Sachs Global Economics Papers, N° 66, November 30, 2001.

17 Michael Cox, "Too Big To Fail? The Transatlantic Relationship from Bush to Obama", Global Policy, Vol. 3, 2012, p. 76.

18 Kristian Nielsen, "Continued Drift, but Without the Acrimony: US-European Relations under Barack Obama", Journal of Transatlantic Studies, 11:1, 2013, p. 100.

19 PRISM (Planning Tool for Resource Integration, Synchronization and Management) is claimed to be the biggest downstream surveillance program collecting data directly from the servers of some of the biggest US Internet provider companies including AOL, Apple, Facebook, Google, Microsoft, PalTalk, Skype Yahoo and You Tube.

20 Mark Leonard, "The Long Tail of the Snowden Saga", The State of the Transatlantic World, Transatlantic Academy, April 2014, p. 5.

tions were contradictory. For instance, the Resolution voted by the European Parliament in October 2013 that was calling for the suspension of the US-EU Terrorist Finance Tracking Program (TFTP) was rejected by the Commission. Member states' reactions in response to the NSA revelations also varied significantly from one state to another. France and Germany where the public debate was really heated, announced they would seek new bilateral arrangements with the US to impose some strict regulations on their respectful surveillance activities. Germany even went further by suggesting that a bilateral "no-spy" agreement could be signed with the US but this proposal was refused by Washington. Other EU member states' reactions were more limited as the one of the UK, which could easily be explained by the disclosure about the British national surveillance services' complicity with the NSA.

NSA revelations actually provoked not just a new transatlantic drift. It was also about a crisis of trust in the transatlantic partnership caused by the breach of EU citizens' right to privacy and data protection by US surveillance agencies in the name of security measures. Solving this crisis seems complicated because it hinges upon understanding and bridging the gap between two fundamentally different approaches of balancing between national security and civil liberties. On the one hand, the European approach that is based on EU member states' constant efforts to strike the right balance between privacy and security. On the other hand, the American approach that tends to give priority to national security, even if it means violating privacy and data protection rights[21]. While the PRISM scandal revealed that the legal asymmetries between the EU and the US data protection laws were deeper than expected and could therefore hamper the transatlantic cooperation in the security field, especially regarding the fight against terrorism and serious crime, it also raised consciousness about the need for urgent reforms of the data protection legislation on both sides of the Atlantic. In this regard, reforms concerning the US surveillance system have recently been announced by president Obama, while the European Commission keeps on working on the Data Protection reform as well as on the Umbrella Agreement that was launched in 2011 as a frame-

---

21 Claude Moraes, "Working Document on the relation between the surveillance practices in the EU and the US and the EU data protection provisions", in: LIBE Committee Inquiry, Electronic Mass Surveillance of EU Citizens 2013- 2014, European Parliament, p. 96.

work agreement with the US on data protection in the area of police and judicial cooperation.

Phase Five: the Rapprochement

What shifted the focus of attention from the PRISM scandal, thus making the US and the EU act again in tandem, was the crisis in Ukraine that began in November 2013 when pro-Russian President Viktor Yanukovych decided to break Ukraine's EU association agreement negotiations in favour of stronger ties with Russia resulting in the signature of a free trade agreement between the two countries. This decision triggered social protests in the capital Kiev causing the fall of Yanukovych's regime defined as a "coup d'état" by Russia. In reaction to this, Pro-Russian separatist protests arose in Crimea where the majority of the population is ethnic Russian. Pro-Russian insurgents took advantage of the chaos to seize key government buildings. The Referendum organized by the Parliament was a sheer success with 97% of all voters backing up the proposal to join Russia. Despite some US-EU differences at the beginning as to what sanctions to be applied against Russia – the Europeans taking a more reserved stance towards Moscow because of the dependence of some EU countries on Russian oil and gas supplies, both the US and the EU officials condemned the annexation of Crimea and imposed the first economic sanctions on Russia in March 2014 that were enhanced in July and September 2014 targeting Russia's financial, defense and energy sectors.

Although the US-EU cooperation demonstrated a renewed transatlantic cooperation, some observers argue that the sanctions are not completely harmonized depending on the interests that each side of the Atlantic has with regard to Russia, which might make US-EU tensions resurface, especially if some EU member states start pressing to withdraw certain sanctions if a ceasefire in Ukraine is respected by Moscow[22].

Another case of expected rapprochement between the US and its European allies is the US-led military intervention against the fundamentalist group Islamic state (IS) controlling much of eastern Syria and western Iraq, that both American and European officials defined as an imminent

---

22 Kristin Archick and Derek Mix, "US-EU Cooperation on Ukraine and Russia", CRS Insights, September 16, 2014.

threat for the transatlantic and the international security. However, intra-European and transatlantic differences appeared again since some EU countries, such as Germany, decided not to participate in the military operation, while others put in doubt the efficiency of the US-pursued strategy of arming Syrian rebel forces to fight the IS on the frontline.

Last but not least, even the case concerning Iran's nuclear program on which Americans and Europeans have jointly been working for quite some time now, contain some subtle differences in the EU and US positions. While the Europeans tend to "play by the rules" by using only diplomatic means for pressure on Teheran, the Americans are conducting a cyberwar against Iran begun by Bush, but accelerated by Obama, that aims at attacking the computer systems running Iran's main nuclear enrichment facilities[23].

The above-made analysis contends that transatlantic relations under Obama's Presidency cannot simply be qualified in terms of success or failure. Indeed, they were marked by ups and downs depending mostly on systemic factors, i.e. external factors related to the "global power shift", the global economic crisis and the emergence of new threats on the international scene. For sure, Obama has not been the "Atlantic president" that Europeans dreamt for. Moreover, he never tried to conceal his boredom concerning the EU institutions' heavy bureaucracy and complicated functioning, as well as his feeling of unease when discussing every time with a different representative of the EU on global issues instead of being given "Europe's phone number" and being always put through to the same person. Nevertheless, thanks to his pragmatic and smart diplomacy-oriented foreign policy approach, Obama managed to improve transatlantic relations and make the transatlantic partnership work, especially in hard economic times and in the context of "hot cases" such as the crisis in Ukraine and the rise of the Islamic state, representing an imminent threat for the European and American security that need a quick and efficient joint plan and action.

(published online mid-December 2014)

---

23 David Sager, "Obama Order Sped up Wave of Cyber Attacks against Iran", The New York Times, June 1, 2012.

International affairs

Formal and Informal Institutions and Economic Development - comparative research

Ryszard Piasecki

In the Washington Consensus, which was adopted in the 1980's and 1990's by many developing and former communist countries, apart from capital inflows, deregulation, liberalization and privatization were considered to be of key significance. Openness and privatization strategies in the last 25 years have become worldwide processes covering many countries. This process has had many elements of universal significance, but there have also been many elements specific to a particular group of countries sharing a similar socio – economic structure and a certain position in the world economy.

In the period 2008-2014 I conducted research on development processes in the underdeveloped and medium developed countries in the Central and Eastern Europe, South America, Asia and Africa.[1] Several important conclusions can be drawn from that analysis:

- Undoubtedly reforms to the public sector and privatization prevented the establishment of other ineffective state-owned enterprises. Mere privatization, however, without the creation of a competitive environment and effective pro-market institutions could not fulfill the hopes which were placed on it.
- In many countries the institutional system turned out to be either inefficient (Latin America except for Chile, Asia) or non-existent (Africa). • General insecurity and instability in such areas as property rights or copyright make economic subjects unwilling to get involved in long-term enterprises, resulting in a lack of necessary investment in fixed assets.
- The example of some countries (e.g. Indonesia, Argentina) shows that even positive economic parameters are not able to prevent financial and state crises. A political crisis, or rather a sociopolitical crisis, is as dangerous as an upset in the macroeconomic balance. It leads to the

---

1 R. Piasecki, Rozwój gospodarczy, PWE, Warszawa 2011.

loss of those investment activities requiring confidence in the authorities in a given country. The fragility of this trust is particularly obvious in countries with widespread corruption, nepotism and so called "crony" capitalism. The market is ineffective where conditions are weak or where the necessary financial, social, legal or political infrastructure is lacking.

- The example of other countries (e.g. Argentina) shows that market reforms should be a natural consequence of the broadening of market freedom. This country is a good example of how market transformation has little effect if institutional reforms are not realized, if there are no competitive conditions and if corruption and nepotism are not limited.

- In the researched countries one can confirm the theory that effective institutional and legal systems are of key significance for development. These countries have weak state and legal institutions. Their distinct setback is the lack of structural reforms, huge income stratification, fragile investors' confidence and corruption. The thesis of lack of discipline, poor organization, low or inadequate education and knowledge of society can also be confirmed.

- Chile is a good example of an emerging economy with effective institutions (law abiding country, respect for property rights, no corruption) which is developing quite quickly.

- With the example of the researched countries it can be argued that a strong state is necessary particularly with respect to the formation of institutions and providing for their effectiveness.

Nobel Prize winner Douglas C North (1993) wrote in the World Bank report that it was essential to motivate people, so that they would want to invest in better technologies, increase their capacities and organize effective markets. Such motivation is placed in institutions. What primarily differentiates rich countries from poor ones is the existence and quality of certain institutions. By this I do not mean governments creating new bureaucratic bodies, government agencies, commissions or institutions. The institutions supporting the market do not have to be public and they do not even have to be formalized.

The most important tasks of institutions include: lowering transaction costs, the costs of launching new products and facilitating access to information. The institutional environment of the market acquires key significance when the issue of transaction costs is taken into account. It is known that the play of supply and demand depends on the level of social confidence and the transparency of functional conditions. These are influenced by the quality of the system, the moral principles and mentality of economic subjects. In other words, market effectiveness, and consequently, the level of transaction costs, depends on the institutions. Institutions and transaction costs are the two deciding factors of market effectiveness.

D. Rodrik from Harvard divides the system of market institutions into four basic categories:

- market – creating institutions, such as property rights, rights guaranteeing contract execution
- market regulating institutions – such as external effects, production scale, information about company activities, etc.
- market – stabilizing institutions – such as monetary and fiscal policy management, etc.
- market – legitimizing institutions, such as social protection, insurances, etc.[2]

According to the World Bank institutions can be divided into public and private ones. The public institutions include the legal and court systems, property rights, copyright, inheritance law, rights regulating and protecting competition as well as the "transparency" of government institutions and private enterprises. The private institutions include: trade chambers, loan and loaner registers, principles of inheriting land, mutuality of business partners, etc.

For the market to function properly there must be an effective legal – institutional infrastructure, the system must be transparent and property rights must be guaranteed. The better the guarantee of property rights and the better the system of debt execution, the easier it is for companies to do business for companies. Strong institutions are particularly important for smaller and weaker subjects. Corruption and poor debt execution are plagues resulting in increased transaction costs. Institutions providing for reliable contracts are a necessary condition for effective markets, underpinning the foundations of rich societies. Institutional stability is a condition for exchange in space and time. A lack of conditions for concluding

---

2 D. Rodrick, A Thousand Growth Model Bloom, Project Syndicate, J.F. Kennedy School of Government, Harvard University, April 2002.

reliable contracts is a primary cause of stagnation both in developing and in former socialist countries.

Economists agree that **competition** is the best stimulus for economic development. The role of the state should include competition protection and drawing up effective regulations in this area. It is the law that is the most important state institution supporting the market. The more effective it is, the lower transaction costs are for enterprises. An effective market economy should be the main drive of any development strategy but its final success depends on effective competition policy and an effective legal – institutional system. Deregulation, liberalization and privatization serve to achieve those goals, but their effectiveness is limited if they are not accompanied by complementary reforms.

At present economists dealing with economic development generally agree with the following opinions:

- Existing development models were rather shortterm ones and as such they have often led to negative results. It means that a long- term perspective has key significance for economic development.
- Investments in human and social capital have fundamental significance for success in long-term development.
- Institutions determine developmental efforts, and current solutions in this field in developing countries are not sufficient or even anti-developmental. The adaptation of institutional system (it's worth remembering that the market itself is an institution) to meet the requirements of market economy has key significance.
- Cultural conditions of individual countries should be analyzed in more detail; in some case they seem decisive.
- An incentive system for both for individuals and the whole of society is essential as well as including these solutions into developmental policy;
- The private sector has key significance for economic development but the role of the state should not be neglected (legal system should help competition, subsidies should develop necessary physical infrastructure and so on).

There is no agreement, however, among development economists in the following issues:

- Methods of reducing poverty and general economic growth acceleration;
- Role of state in initiating developmental processes (top-bottom interventionism or a bigger role for liberal individual choices even at a price of growing social inequalities).
- Role of political factors in developmental processes
- What is the best way of mobilizing social support for development of human capital in a given country, population programs, physical and information infrastructure development, formation of proper financial institutions, as well as for the issues of exchange rate policy, inflation objectives, international capital flow, etc..

Of course a question arises if the experience of other countries, particularly of medium developed ones, has relevance to Central and Eastern Europe. Undoubtedly, we deal with different economic, political, social, institutional and cultural conditions. It is not easy to transfer institutional systems from one country to the other, as in each country there are individual cultural circumstances. Nevertheless, in all analyzed countries there are striking experience similarities related to economy liberalization.

Firstly, privatization without effective competition does not fulfill the expectations which were placed on it.

Secondly, an effective legal – institutional infrastructure is necessary. A pro-market institution system seems to have a key significance for economic development. At the same time fundamental importance is attached to the effectiveness of institutions which create, protect and execute laws (which must be logical and coherent). The whole system of social institutions must also act effectively. In this area the state must be strong and efficient.

Thirdly, in the era of information society, the development of a knowledge – based economy has key significance.

Fourthly, corruption and nepotism, similar to the lack of political stability, lead to the loss of trust among investors.

Fifthly, cultural factors may play an important role in braking or accelerating development. Thus, the general education of society plays a fundamental role in overcoming cultural barriers.

Undoubtedly these conclusions may be fully relevant to our post communist situation. At the present level of economic development, particular significance should be attributed to the creation of a competitive environment, cultural factors (including mentality changes), to fighting against corruption and nepotism and the formation of effective pro market institutions.

In the implementation of those tasks in the post communist member states, the mature institutional system of the European Union (through the adoption of acquis communautaire) has already played a particularly positive role. Effective adaptation of the EU institutional system seems to be much more important than the financial assistance.

(published online mid-April 2015)

Pauvreté dans l'espace Euro-MENA: au-delà de mare nostrum quelle politique de développement Euro-MENA?

Arnaud Leconte

Introduction

La pauvreté est multidimensionnelle. Dans sa définition la plus simple, elle caractérise le manque de revenu du ménage (ou de consommation) en mesure absolue. Le seuil correspond en général à un panier de consommation avec une ration calorique minimale. L'Europe fait exception avec un seuil relatif, équivalant à 60% du revenu médian. Concrè- tement, à l'exemple de la France étant donné que le niveau de vie médian est en 2015 de 1.645 euros par mois, 60% de cette somme correspond à un seuil de pauvreté de 987 euros.

En revanche les Etats-Unis ou le Canada ne sont pas sur cette logique. Ils utilisent un seuil absolu, niveau de revenu en dessous duquel ils estiment qu'on ne peut plus manger, s'habiller et se loger de manière à rester en bonne santé. Aux Etats-Unis par exemple, pour une personne seule, le seuil de pauvreté est l'équivalent de 910 euros. Ainsi, même le seuil "absolu" varie avec la richesse des pays. La Banque mondiale a choisi 1,25 dollar par jour en parité de pouvoir d'achat ajusté $ US de 2005, moyenne des seuils des quinze pays les plus pauvres. Le taux de pauvreté par tête mesure la proportion de ménages dans un pays vivant en dessous de ce seuil de pauvreté international.

Plus généralement, la pauvreté signifie l'incapacité de répondre aux besoins de base, notamment la nourriture, des abris, des vêtements, de l'eau et de l'assainissement, l'éducation et les soins de santé. En ce sens, la pauvreté reflète généralement une combinaison de la pauvreté sur le revenu au niveau du ménage et de la pauvreté au niveau de la communauté dans la fourniture des infrastructures de base et les services publics. En principe, une carte complète de la pauvreté serait d'identifier les personnes vivant dans la pauvreté en raison des faibles revenus des ménages ou des services communautaires inadéquats, et permettrait d'identifier des solutions ciblées à la pauvreté fondée sur la nature précise de la pauvreté. Ce type d'analyse peut être fait au niveau local et national, mais les données requises n'existent pas au niveau mondial.

Pauvreté relative en Europe

Depuis la crise, les écarts de richesse se creusent dangereusement en Europe. Très fortement touchés par la récession, les pays du Sud ont décroché par rapport à ceux du cœur et du Nord du continent. De 2008 à 2013, le nombre de personnes pauvres a beaucoup augmenté au Sud du Continent, passant de 3 millions à 3,9 millions en Grèce (+30%), de 11,1 à 12,6 millions en Espagne, ou encore de 15 à 17,3 millions en Italie. En Grèce, la pauvreté continue à augmenter et touche ainsi plus de 30% de la population en 2015. L'Europe de l'Est, qui a échappé à la crise des dettes souveraines, s'en sort mieux. De 2008 à 2013, le nombre de personnes en difficulté est ainsi passé de 11,5 à 9,7 millions en Pologne, et de 9,4 à 8,6 millions en Roumanie. La France est dans une position intermédiaire: la pauvreté a augmenté sans flamber (de 11,1 à 11,2 millions de personnes). La pauvreté a même augmenté en Allemagne, pourtant première économie de la zone euro, pour atteindre son plus haut niveau depuis la Réunification en 1990, passant de 15% en 2012 à 15,5% en 2013 (12,1 millions de personnes en 2012, 12,5 millions en 2013, pour une population totale de 80 millions d'habitants). Familles monoparentales, retraités et de nombreux mineurs sont les plus touchés. 43% des familles monoparentales et presque 60% des chômeurs sont classés comme pauvres, avec un revenu inférieur à 60% du revenu médian.

La nette réduction des écarts de richesse entre l'Europe du Sud et celle du Nord, qui a eu lieu de 2000 à 2008, n'était pas soutenable. En effet, pendant cette période, les salaires et les dépenses sociales ont augmenté en Espagne, au Portugal ou en Grèce, sans que la productivité ne progresse. Résultat, la compétitivité de ces pays s'est dégradée, ce qui a été un des facteurs déclenchants de la crise. Les politiques de redressement des comptes publics mises en œuvre dans ces pays ont aggravé les choses. Certes, ces pays ont mené des réformes structurelles, sur le marché du travail, les retraites. Mais ils ont aussi coupé dans les dépenses de santé et d'éducation, qui préparent l'avenir: de 2008 à 2012, les dépenses par élève ont baissé de 7% en Grèce et de près de 4% en Espagne. L'accès à la santé s'est souvent dégradé. En 2012, 8% des Grecs n'ont pas pu avoir un examen ou un traitement médical comme cela aurait été nécessaire, contre

5,4% en 2008. Du fait de cette baisse des dépenses dites d'investissement social, les pays d'Europe du Sud sont les plus exposés à un risque d'affaiblissement de leur potentiel de croissance, dont une érosion de leur capital humain. En tous cas, les objectifs que s'étaient fixés les pays de l'Union en 2010 pour l'horizon 2020 en terme de réduction de la pauvreté et de hausse de l'emploi (sortir au moins 20 millions de personnes de la pauvreté et de l'exclusion sociale à l'horizon 2020) risquent fort de ne pas être atteints. Or la convergence des niveaux de vie était bien un des objectifs de la construction européenne.

Où vivent les plus démunis?

En utilisant la mesure de la pauvreté monétaire extrême de la Banque mondiale, environ 1,2 milliard de personnes vivent dans l'extrême pauvreté. Environ 26%vivent dans des pays à faible revenu, principalement dans le Sous-Sahel, selon la classification de la Banque mondiale (moins de $ 1025 PIB par personne en 2011). La forte proportion (74%) des pauvres vivants dans les pays à revenu intermédiaire tels que la Chine, l'Inde et l'Indonésie n'est pas tout à fait surprenante, étant donné que les pays à revenu intermédiaire représentent environ 86% de la population du monde en développement. Les pays avec des revenus moyens faibles qui sont le foyer de la plus grande proportion de personnes pauvres du monde ne sont pas sortis une fois pour toute de la zone des pays où l'extrême pauvreté peut être endémique. Le Nigéria, et beaucoup de pays du Sahel font face à d'énormes défis pour maintenir une croissance économique haute et inclusive, compte tenu de l'évolution démographique, de l'environnement, et de facteurs sociaux très difficiles.

L'Afrique subsaharienne reste la région la plus pauvre du monde et celle avec le plus haut taux de pauvreté extrême (environ 48%). Le Moyen Orient et l'Afrique du Nord représente une part beaucoup plus faible de 0,7% et diffusé surtout dans les parties isolées des centres urbains. Ces zones de pauvreté posent de graves défis humanitaires et sociaux pour les personnes et les lieux concernés, et sont une grande proportion du défi européen global.

Région	Afrique Sub-Saharienne	Asie du Sud	Asie de l'Est	Amérique Latine et Caraïbes	Moyen Orient et Afrique du Nord	Monde
Millions de Pauvres	376	546,5	265,4	35,3	8,5	1 233,8
% des pauvres par rapport à la population mondiale	30,5	44,3	21,5	2,9	0,7	100
% d'extrême Pauvreté par rapport à la population de la région	47,5	36	14,3	6,9	2,7	22,8

Quand on observe dans tous les indicateurs de la pauvreté , dans le tableau 2 , l'Afrique sub-saharienne (avec l'Asie du Sud) est un des deux centres de la pauvreté mondiale et les deux régions exigeants le plus un soutien international . De ces deux régions, l'Afrique subsaharienne, à plus faible revenu que l'Asie du Sud, fait face à des défis et des besoins plus critiques. Alors que les deux régions représentent environ 45% de la population des pays en développement, ils représentent pour une proportion beaucoup plus élevée de la pauvreté dans ses diverses manifestations, généralement bien plus de 70%:

- 75% de la pauvreté de revenu
- 63% de la faim chronique
- 72 % des enfants de l'école
- 75% des adultes analphabètes
- 86% des personnes vivant avec le VIH / SIDA
- 94% + des décès dus au paludisme
- 84% de la mortalité des moins de 5
- 86% de la mortalité maternelle
- 87% de ceux qui pratiquent la défécation en plein air
- 73 % des enfants chétifs

Nous soulignons le caractère approximatif de ces calculs, étant donné les nombreuses incertitudes dans les données sousjacentes .

Causes fondamentales de la pauvreté

Les nombreuses causes fondamentales de la pauvreté extrême comprennent:

1. (Les condition géographiques défavorables: La Corne de l'Afrique et du Sahel sont des exemples de régions où les conditions géographiques très défavorables: enclavés, généralement dépourvu de combustibles fossiles, hyper -arides et sujet à la sécheresse et aux maladies tropicales endémiques, notamment le paludisme et la méningite.

2. un conflit violent prolongé et des sanctions internationales L'incidence de l'extrême pauvreté est fortement corrélée avec les conflits violents et de l'instabilité. La Syrie est réduite à la misère du fait de cinq années de conflit presque continu. De même, l'économie de l'Erythrée a été ravagée par une dictature et des épisodes répétés de sanctions internationales.

3. le gouvernement despotique et la mauvaise gouvernance La mauvaise gouvernance, y compris des niveaux élevés de corruption et une mauvaise allocation des ressources au détriment des besoins des pauvres d'un pays, sont un déterminant important de l'extrême pauvreté. L'Egypte est le cas par excellence de la règle despotique menant à l'extrême pauvreté, malgré le potentiel économique favorable. Le non-respect par certains des pays riches en ressources naturelles en Afrique du Nord comme l'Algérie d'utiliser leur richesse afin de surmonter les inconvénients d'une géographie défavorable est un autre exemple de la mauvaise gouvernance. Plutôt que de servir l'investissement, la rente pétrolière algérienne, plus de 35% du PIB en 2013, a financé le budget courant. Or, les réserves pétrolières s'épuisent et le prix du pétrole à 70 dollars le baril ne couvre plus les dépenses algériennes. Les généraux, qui s'approprient les richesses énergétiques aux dépens du reste de la population, parent au plus pressé en approvisionnant les villes. L'Algérie est ainsi devenue le deuxième importateur mondial de blé en 2015.

4. le genre et la discrimination ethniques ou sociale Les peuples autochtones (environ 400 millions dans le monde) et d'autres groupes exclus ont été confrontés à des siècles de discrimination extrême et l'exclusion sociale. En conséquence, ils ont tendance à vivre dans les parties les plus reculées du pays (géographie défavorable voir ci-dessus) et constituent une proportion particulièrement élevée de l'extrême pauvreté, en

particulier en Asie. Les filles et les femmes continuent d'être victimes de discrimination extrême dans les pratiques sociales et les droits juridiques (par exemple le droit à un titre de propriété) dans de nombreuses régions du monde, ce qui augmente le risque d'extrême pauvreté pour les ménages.

5. Les taux de fécondité extrêmes (6 ou plus) Les zones rurales dans de nombreuses parties de l'Afrique subsaharienne ont des taux de fécondité total de 6 ou plus. Ces taux élevés résultent de la culture (principes religieux, discrimination entre les sexes), l'absence de la scolarisation des filles, une mortalité infantile élevée (conduisant à des choix de fécondité élevé des ménages), et l'indisponibilité des contraceptifs et des services de planification familiale. De hauts taux de fécondité sont l'un des plus importants déterminants de la pauvreté extrê- me, car ils réduisent l'investissement des ménages dans la santé et l'éducation de ses enfants, ainsi que les investissements par habitant du gouvernement dans les infrastructures et les services sociaux qui peuvent réduire la pauvreté.

6. Le manque d'accès à la terre La plupart des ruraux pauvres en Afrique possèdent trop peu des terres. Le manque d'accès à la terre et un manque d'activité lucrative et de possibilités d'emploi peuvent constituer un élément important de l'extrême pauvreté.

Stratégie anti-pauvreté dans un monde globalisé

Les objectifs post-2015 des Nations Unies incluent l'ambition de mettre fin à l'extrême pauvreté. C'est certainement faisable d'ici à 2030. Entre 1990 et 2010, le Taux de Haute Pauvreté (THP) dans le monde en développement est passé d'environ 44% à 22%. Les conditions pour la réduction de la THP proche de zéro sont favorables si les stratégies sont bien conçues et mises en place.

La nature de la pauvreté et les implications politiques sont un peu différentes dans le cas de personnes pauvres dans les pays à faible revenu (en Afrique subsaharienne principalement), et au Moyen Orient et en Afrique du Nord. Dans le cas de personnes pauvres dans les pays pauvres, le gouvernement national n'a pas la base de ressources intérieures pour briser le piège de la pauvreté sur leur propre sol. En outre, il ne peut y avoir quelques opportunités pour soulager la pauvreté grâce à la migration interne des régions pauvres vers les régions riches au sein du pays (comme dans les zones rurales pauvres vers les zones urbaines dynamiques). Dans le cas de gens pauvres vivant dans les pays à revenu intermédiaire, en revanche, les gouvernements disposent davantage de ressources domestiques pour investir dans la réduction de la pauvreté, et il s'offre plus de possibilités aussi bien de migration interne, généralement des zones rurales vers les zones urbaines.

Les tendances et niveaux de sous-alimentation en Afrique du Nord sont très différents de celles dans le reste du continent. La région a atteint des niveaux au-dessous de 5% selon les projections pour 2014-16. Selon les tendances actuelles, la région est proche de l'éradication de l'insécurité alimentaire sévère. L'accès subventionné à l'alimentation est un élément central de la politique dans la région, avec des prix des aliments de base qui reste faible dans de nombreux pays, même lorsque les prix mondiaux connaissent des pics. Tandis que la durabilité de ces mesures peut être mise en doute, ils ont a contribué à maintenir les niveaux de sous-alimentation faible, en fournissant de grande quantité de calories à moindre coût. L'accent sur les calories, cependant, a laissé les problèmes de qualité alimentaires largement négligée, donnant lieu à d'autres formes de malnutrition, dont la prévalence du surpoids et de l'obésité. En outre, la région demeure exposée à l'instabilité politique et économique. Certains pays sont fortement dépendants des importations de produits alimentaires, et leur base de ressources limitées, couplé avec la croissance rapide de la population, suggère que la dépendance des importations restera une caractéristique de la région dans le futur, malgré les efforts pour accroître la productivité agricole.

En Afrique sub-saharienne, moins d'un sur quatre personnes, ou 23,2% de la population d'après la FAO, est estimée être sous-alimentées sur la période 2014-16. Ceci est la plus forte prévalence de sous-alimentation pour toute la région et, avec environ 220 millions de personnes affamées en 2014-16, le deuxième plus lourd fardeau en termes absolus. En fait, le nombre de personnes sous-alimentées a même augmenté de plus de 20 millions entre 2005-2007 et 2014-16. Cette augmentation reflète le taux de croissance de la population remarquablement élevé de la région de 2,7% par an. La lenteur des progrès dans lutte contre la faim au cours des années est particulièrement inquiétante. Alors que la famine est tombée assez rapidement entre 2000-02 et 2005-07, ce rythme a ralenti dans les années suivantes, reflétant des facteurs tels que la hausse des prix alimentaires, les sécheresses et politique instabilité dans plusieurs pays.

L'Afrique subsaharienne est confrontée à un énorme fardeau de besoins d'investissement, de construction d'infrastructures de base (électricité, routes, rail, eau et assainissement, de la fibre optique, et plus encore), ainsi que la nécessité de surmonter les déficits d'énergie, le fardeau de la maladie, de l'irrigation, et d'autres vulnérabilités aux changements climatiques. Un taux de fécondité excessive signifie que l'Afrique sub-saharienne de population, autour de 856 millions (2010), est sur une trajectoire de dépasser les 3,3 milliards en 2100, sur la base de prévision moyenne de fécondité de l'ONU. Une population proche ou à ce niveau signifierait la dévastation des écosystèmes et de ses habitants pauvres de l'Afrique, en particulier face à des risques croissants du changement climatique induit par l'homme.

Hautement prioritaires les défis anti-pauvreté de la région comprennent:

- Le financement des infrastructures (électricité, routes, rail, eau et assainissement)
- La couverture des soins de santé universels
- La réduction des taux de fécondité au-dessous de 3,0 (à partir d'une moyenne actuelle de 4,8, et beaucoup plus élevé dans les zones rurales)
- L'accès universel à l'éducation à travers le niveau secondaire
- Mise à niveau de l'agriculture rurale par le soutien aux petits agriculteurs
- Amélioration de la gouvernance et la responsabilité de rendre ce qui précède possible

Tous ces éléments sont une action pratique et réalisable. Ensemble, ils permettront à l'Afrique à la fois rurale et urbaine à sortir du piège de la pauvreté.

Toutefois, la transition démographique africaine se fait dans un monde globalisé bien différent du 19ème et du 20ème siècle. La région MENA est soumise à des défis inconnus que sont le changement climatique et l'évolution globale des prix des matières premières et des biens et services. Par le passé, les migrations des régions rurales en Europe et en Asie ont été absorbées par les secteurs industriels et le tertiaire. En retour, la hausse des prix des matières agricoles pour nourrir les villes a permis aux campagnes de bénéficier des transferts économiques et sociaux des villes. Au XXIème siècle, la concurrence agricole globale met les paysans d'Afrique en concurrence avec les prix agricoles faibles, par exemple le riz importé d'Asie. La ruralité africaine ne bénéficie pas d'une hausse des prix des matières pour alimenter les villes. Les biens et services eux-mêmes sont soumis à des prix mondiaux, qui ne permettent pas aux secteurs industriels et tertiaires de transférer localement leurs gains de productivité. Or, l'Europe est en forte concurrence avec la Chine dans la région MENA. Le Programme chinois de développement de l'Afrique mis en place en 2006 répond à une grande attente des pays africains. La Chine a mis en place des centres de démonstration agricoles, construit des infrastructures de transport et d'énergie. La sécurité alimentaire du continent est une préoccupation majeure de la Chine, certains d'iront pour sécuriser les investissements chinois et garantir un accès stratégique aux ressources africaines. En 2015 la Chine est très perméable aux problématiques démographiques africaines. Lors du prochain Forum de coopération Chine-Afrique en Juillet 2015 il faut s'attendre à une réorientation de la politique chinoise prenant en compte la nécessaire transition démographique de l'Afrique.

Nouvelle stratégie de développement Euro-MENA

Au-delà des faibles financements que l'Europe parvient difficilement à mobiliser dans ses opérations de lutte contre l'immigration en Mer Méditerranée, l'Europe doit mettre en place une nouvelle stratégie de développement euro-MENA.

Les gros titres des journaux en Europe sur l'immigration massive en Mer Méditerranée s'affranchissent de la réalité de migrations intra-africaines et Afrique-Moyen Orient aussi importantes que les migrations Afrique-Europe. Si l'Italie, l'Espagne et la Grèce reçoivent des flots d'émigrants, d'autres pôles d'attraction en Afrique sont plus simples, moins dangereux dans des zones régionales de libre-circulation pour les personnes. L'Afrique sub-saharienne compte ainsi plus de 3 millions de réfugiés et le seul Liban accueille un million de réfugiés syriens, qui représentent 25% de la population.

Les migrations sont pour la moitié intra-africaine, marquées par la solidarité ethnique, beaucoup dans les pays du Golfe depuis les années 2000 et dans les pays d'Afrique du Nord (Maroc, Tunisie, Algérie, moins en Lybie depuis la guerre et l'instabilité chronique de la politique lybienne). L'Afrique a plus de 100 ans de tradition de départ et d'émigration (Mauritanie, Sénégal, Burkina-Faso, Afrique du Nord) bénéficiant des redistributions des émigrés. La migration vers l'Afrique du Nord est marquée par l'ambition diplomatique du Maroc dans toute l'Afrique Sub-saharienne.

L'insécurité, le risque pays, et le manque de confiance dans le gouvernement poussent les classes moyennes et aisées, plus que les plus pauvres à partir. De part la pression démographique, le développement économique doit permettre de créer 29 Millions d'emplois en Afrique tous les ans d'ici 2030. Or si la zone du Nigéria-Libéria est marquée par une urbanisation dense, l'espace sub-saharien est caractérisé par une absence de liens entre les zones et une construction territoriale qui maintient les déséquilibres.

Les facteurs critiques de développement sont ainsi le peuplement (pression dans les villes et dans les campagnes sur le foncier, dangereux pour l'équilibre social), et l'aménagement du territoire et de rééquilibrage territorial, pas assez pris en compte dans l'aide au développement.

La politique de développement doit s'éloigner d'une approche verticale et sectorielle. Ce diagnostic est partagé par les acteurs, mais la mise en place d'une politique du peuplement de d'aménagement du territoire est extrêmement lente, à l'image de l'absence complète de la CDAO près du lac Tchad où la secte Boko Haram étend sa présence.

La politique publique européenne d'aide au développement reste peu ambitieuse et faite au sommet. L'objectif d'une aide publique au développement de 0,7% du PNB établi dans les années 60, n'est toujours pas respecté, notamment par la France. Les fonds publics doivent avoir un effet catalytique et d'entrainement. Nous assistons à une montée des fonds privés d'investissement pour des partenariats publics-privés dont de nombreux fonds africains. Les fonds privés d'investissement ont de nombreux projets, mais ciblent des investissements à valeur ajoutée privée et sectorielle.

Or la politique de développement doit dépasser les stratégies sectorielles. La vision d'une agriculture très productiviste ayant comme seul objet l'auto-suffisance, doit être complétée par la mise en place d'une filière agricole décentralisée. Les variétés de plantes fourragères qui résistent à la semi-aridité de la steppe ne sont pas encore sélectionnées et produites dans la région MENA. Le retard est encouragé par le lobby des importateurs d'aliments pour bétail provenant d'Europe.

Dans un monde globalisé, la politique de développement Euro-MENA ne dispose plus de recette miracle voulant soit mettre le paquet sur l'agriculture (comme le Brésil), soit sur l'industrialisation avec le renforcement des économies industrielle (comme la Chine), soit sur les services (comme l'Inde). Elle doit faire tout en même temps et avoir une approche multi-sectorielle, participative, et territorialisée. Elle doit combler l'absence d'outils financiers de solidarité intergénérationnel et permettre à l'Europe de définir son identité comme terre d'immigration.

Tableau 2: Indicateurs sélectionnés de pauvreté

Nombre (% du monde)	Afrique Sub-Saharienne	Asie du Sud	Afrique Sub-Saharienne et Asie du Sud, Sous-total	Moyen Orient et Afrique du Nord	World
Revenu en dessous du seuil de pauvreté (1,25 $), (en millions)	376 (31)	546.5 (44)	922.5 (75)	8.5 (1)	1233.8 (100)
Famine 2005-07 (en millions)	206 (26,5)	319,1 (20,1)	525,1 (46,7)	7 (<5)	942,3 (14,3)
Famine 2014-2016 (projections) (en millions)	220 (23,2)	281,4 (15,7)	501,4 (38,9)	4,3 (<5)	794,6 (10,9)
Enfants en dehors de l'école, 2008 (en millions)	28.9 (45)	16.9** (26)	45.8 (72)	7.2 (11)	67.5 (100)
Adulte analphabète 2005-8 (en millions)	167.2 (21)	412.4 (inclus l'Asie de l'Ouest) (53)	589.6 (75)	60.2 (8)	795.8 (100)
Personnes vivant avec le VIH, 2011 (en millions)	23.5 (77)	2.6* (9)	26.1 (86)	0.3 (1)	34.2 (100)
Décès dûs au paludisme (000s)	596 (91)	20* (3)	616 (94)	15 (2)	655 (100)
Mortalité des enfants de moins de cinq ans, 2011 (000s)	3,370 (49)	2,341 (34)	5,711 (84)	314 (5)	6,914 (100)
Mortalité maternelle, 2010 (000s)	162 (57)	83 (29)	245 (86)	7 (2)	287 (100)
Manque d'assainissement ,2010 (défécation en milieu ouvert), (000s)	214 (20)	699 (67)	913 (87)	7 (1)	1,054 (100)
Enfant en retard de croissance, moins de 5 ans , 2006-10, (en millions)	54 (28)	85 (45)	139 (73)	16 (8)	172 (100)

Remarque: % en colonnes peut ne pas correspondre à 100 en raison des arrondis

Sources:

http://www.oecd.org/social/income-distribution-database.htm
Agence des Nations Unies pour les Refugiés
Poverty, Sumner, IDS Working Paper 2012
Hunger, FAO, The State of Food Insecurity in the World 2015, Table 1
School, UNESCO, Education for All Global Monitoring Report 2011
Illiteracy, UNESCO Education for All Global Monitoring Report 2011
Malaria deaths, WHO World Malaria Report, 2011
Child Mortality, Levels and Trends in Child Mortality 2012, United Nations
Maternal Mortality, Trends in Maternal Mortality, 1990-2010, WHO and others
Sanitation, Progress on Drinking Water and Sanitation 2012 Update
Stunting, State of the World's Children 2012, UNICEF

(published online end of June 2015)

List of Authors – Liste des auteurs

Laurent Baechler est économiste, Directeur du Master in European Studies and International Relations (MAEIS) du CIFE filière anglophone, et rédacteur en chef de « L'Europe en formation ». Il est spécialisé dans les questions de développement durable, liées en particulier aux problématiques énergétiques, climatiques et hydriques.

Katrin Böttger est Directrice adjointe de l'Institut de la Politique européenne (Institut für Europäische Politik, IEP, Berlin)), où elle dirige le projet de recherche « La politique européenne à l'égard de l'Europe orientale et de l'Asie centrale : un rôle clé pour l'Allemagne ». Ses champs de recherche principaux à l'IEP sont la politique européenne de voisinage, l'élargissement de l'Union européenne, les relations de l'UE avec l'Asie centrale et le processus constitutionnel de l'UE.

Anna Dimitrova is Associate Professor and Researcher in International relations at ESCE International Business School (Paris.) Holder of the Master in Advanced European and International Studies (MAEIS) of CIFE and a PhD in Sociology at the University Nice of Sophia-Antipolis, she also did a post-doctoral research in Political Science at CNRS (Paris). Her research interests and publications are mainly focused on US foreign policy, transatlantic relations, Euro-Mediterranean relations, and geopolitics and conflicts.

Susann Heinecke is a research associate at CIFE Berlin and programme manager of its PhD Support Programme. She studies political science, cultural studies and journalism and received her doctoral degree in 2011 for a thesis on German Policy towards Russia. Her research interests include foreign policy analysis, German foreign policy, German-Russian relations, and current developments in the CIS region.

András Inotai, professor emeritus, former director (1991-2011) of the Institute for World Economics of the Hungarian Academy of Sciences. Professor at the College of Europe, Natolin (Poland), Center for European Integration at the University of Bonn, European Online Academy (Berlin and Nice). Key research areas include globalization, current and future challenges of the European integration, main areas of economic security and comparative analysis of Central and Eastern European countries (transformation, macroeconomic development, impact of and on the European Union as full-fledged member countries).

Jarosław Jańczak is Assistant Professor at the European University Viadrina, Frankfurt (Oder), Germany and the Adam Mickiewicz University, Poznań, Poland

Mathias Jopp is director of the Institute for European Politics, Berlin. He is Honorary Professor at the University of Tübingen. His main research fields are European foreign relations, EU security and defence politics, and Germany's European politics.

Arnaud Leconte holds a PhD in finance and economics. His main research interests are the Euro-Mediterranean policy and sustainable development.

Hartmut Marhold is CIFE's Director of Research and Development. He is Honorary Professor at the University of Cologne and teaches at the Turkish-German University, Istanbul. His research covers European integration history, EU institutional developments and Germany's European politics.

Philippe Maystadt is former Deputy Prime Minister of Belgium, former President of the European Investment Bank (EIB) and President of CIFE. He teaches at various Belgian and other universities and is involved in the work of different Brussels based think tanks.

Michael Meimeth, political scientist, is Director of the Overseas University Programmes, CIFE.

Ryszard Piasecki is a Polish economist and diplomat, professor at the University of Lodz, recently Ambassador in Chile, member of the board of CIFE.

Funda Tekin chairs CIFE's research projects, in particular the « FEU-TURE » (future of EU-Turkey relations, an EU funded consortium project). She holds a PhD in political science from the University of Cologne, and is an expert in EU differentiated integration.

George N. Tzogopoulos, CIFE Alumnus, is a journalist and media-politics expert. He is founder of chinaandgreece.com and the author of the books US Foreign Policy in the European Media (IB TAURIS 2012) and The Greek Crisis in the Media (Ashgate 2013).

Jean-Claude Vérez, économiste, maître de conférences habilité à diriger des recherches, responsable du module Economie et Mondialisation à l'Institut Européen de Nice.

Matthias Waechter est Directeur général du CIFE. Il a fait son doctorat et son habilitation en histoire, et est professeur associé à l'université de Freiburg. Il est un spécialiste de l'histoire des Etats-Unis, de la France contemporaine, des relations franco-allemandes et de la construction européenne. Dans ses recherches, il se concentre sur des problèmes des identités collectives, de l'imaginaire historique, des mythes politiques et des intellectuels transnationaux.